Football Club United of Manchester, *created from despair - powered by passion*

An Unofficial guide to the North West Counties Years

Michael Beard

Authors
On Line

Visit us online at www.authorsonline.co.uk

This book is written with love and devotion to FC United.

All the work is mine and mine alone except the pictures which belong to Andy Barker.

I have researched the information found with books and scouring by the internet, and have tried my best to make sure the facts are true but I accept that mistakes will be made and if anyone is offended then I apologise.

I am also open to suggestions and comments, so if anyone wants to email me then please do so at: michael@taylor-beard.me.uk.

If any player wants me to omit or add anything or to correct anything then please let me know and I will do my best to make the changes.

It is an *unofficial* guide and hopefully can only get better!

Other books on FC United:

An Undividable Glow by Robert Brady ISBN: 0-9553620-0-8

.

With Thanks:

As with all books nothing could ever happen without help from many people.

My thanks go to my family, Hayley for being the football widow, my sons Karl for supporting FC United with me and accompanying me on those long trips. To Joshua who wishes I would support a 'proper' football team and my youngest Oliver who just wants to play football like Beckham!

To my friends who would wish I would shut up about FC United and to you the fans.

My thanks also go to FC United for the help they have provided, made my job a wee bit easier!

Voxra you are a star amongst stars thank you.

My thanks also go to Andy Barker for supplying the wonderful images including the crowd scene for the covers, I'm sorry I couldn't use more. Check out Andy's web sites:

http://www.fcutdphotos.co.uk or

http://www.andybarkerphotography.com

Salutations and live long you guys!

Football Club United of Manchester

Created from despair - Powered by passion

Preface:

My reasons for wanting to write this book are very simple and yet complex.

Simple because I am passionate about FC United and I desperately want them to be a success, and to my mind they are way beyond a success. I also want to tell the world about the club; the club I helped to create, albeit in a small capacity. Something to tell the grandchildren about!

Complex because it involves emotions of the heart and I'm torn in different directions. First and foremost, I am a Manchester United fan and have been since the days of George Best. But I have not enjoyed, just put up with, the changes inflicted on the club and its treatment of the fans. Over time, these stifling conditions have put limitations on my passion.

You can't have fish without chips or a pub without beer or a football match without fans.

You want to queue up to get into a game; not queue up to see if you're eligible for tickets for a future game. You want to watch the game with your mates and sing and chant; not be told where to sit and to be quiet.

We want the players and managers to appreciate us. *Us*: the people who pay sometimes heavily and whose money allows the players to have a decent wage and look good.

We want the owners to be as passionate about the club as we are and not hide away in a foreign country.

Like many thousands of fans, I bought shares in the club that I love. I wanted to make sure that my club – and that's what it was: *my* club – had funds available to buy the best players, to improve the stadium, have the best training facilities and give me something back in return – enjoyment and ultimately success.

Naively, I didn't expect anyone who did not have Manchester United's best interests at heart to buy the club. Not just to buy the club, but to buy the club knowing that the fans opposed the takeover, buy the club for profit not football and to buy the club knowing that they were not wanted.

For me, the unwanted hostile takeover of Manchester United has taken away the love of football and replaced it with commercialism and emptiness.

So my heart watches the football results to see how Manchester United fare, but if I want to watch a game of football, soak up the atmosphere, scream and shout until the hairs on the back of my neck stand on end, then it's FC United every time. I've paid my money and I've made my choice!

Chapter 1: The Business Years

12th May 2005 – a dark day in Manchester. News had just reached the thousands of Manchester United fans that Malcolm Glazer had won where many had tried and failed in his fight to take over Manchester United. It was news that did not bode well and left many with a bitter taste.

The long, hard, bitter war was finally over and the fans had lost.

The War with Murdoch:

Whether we as Manchester United fans like it or not, Manchester United has been for sale for many years; in fact, a lot longer than we realise.

The club was in financial difficulty as far back as 1902 when it owed £2,670 and was saved from bankruptcy by four local businessmen, including John Henry Davies. They each paid £500 to have a say in the running of the club, which included changing the name to Manchester United.

The lack of pounds, shillings and pence loomed again in 1931, with United again heavily in debt. The club was saved this time by sports lover James W Gibson, who paid the wages of the players and some of the directors. Alas, it was not enough to bring the club back to solvency and so Gibson issued a number of shares to local businessmen and selected fans in order to raise the £20,000 necessary to run the club literally week by week.

Following Gibson's death, the running of the club fell to Louis Edwards.

It was Edwards' burning desire to turn Old Trafford into the best stadium in the country and it was he who masterminded the financial revolution at Manchester United. He raised the number of investors, taking the number from 90 to 2000, and raised over £1m from the new investors.

Being a private club, the shares were not available to the general public and despite the initial boost in funds the team fared little better on the field. The club's lack of success continued when Louis stepped down and his son Martin took the helm.

In 1984, the late newspaper mogul Robert Maxwell tried unsuccessfully to buy Manchester United for £10m, and later, in 1989, Michael Knighton tried and failed in his bid to buy the club, backed by a bitter Robert Maxwell.

It was Martin Edwards who made the club a Public limited company (Plc) on 31st May 31 1991 and raised money to improve Old Trafford and netted millions for himself in the process.

The battle plans had been drawn when Rupert Murdoch attempted to take control in 1998 and the Mergers and Monopolies Commission (MMC) ruled against Murdoch's BSkyB takeover.

The eyes and hearts of the world focused on Rupert Murdoch's battle to control the world's richest club. Sole opposition to this takeover was the Independent Manchester United Supporters Association (IMUSA), an organisation set up by the fans who were not ready to see the greatest club in the world trampled under foot. IMUSA rallied support, hired halls, sent out leaflets and propaganda. An appeal began and raised £40k, with £10k being donated by Roger Taylor from the rock group Queen.

Sky was reliant on the element of surprise and any delay would reveal its plans.

Football Club United of Manchester

Created from despair - Powered by passion

Obtaining a referral to the MMC was crucial for IMUSA and allowed all interested parties to make submissions and give IMUSA a chance of winning.

Before then, those bodies had to be persuaded to make submissions to the Office of Fair Trading (OFT) to get an MMC referral in the first place.

With the OFT involved, the first target was to get the investigation delayed to allow further submissions.

Campaigners attempted to ensure that every organisation and person with influence in sport bombarded the OFT with submissions. These tactics worked so successfully that the OFT fax machine broke down twice and the investigation was delayed. A battle had been won, now for the war!

The fight was also taken to Parliament and an Early Day Motion (EDM) was proposed to focus Parliament's attention on Murdoch's agenda. Manchester MP Terry Brown, who was already a member of IMUSA, lobbied the all-party football group, persuading 200 MPs to sign the EDM.

Submissions to the MMC had been crucial to its decision and the powerful arguments made by the Independent Manchester United Supporters Association (IMUSA) and newly-formed Shareholders United Against Murdoch (SUAM) were made with heavyweight professional advice.

Seven months later the MMC's final report was published. Stephen Byers stated that the takeover could operate against public interest and should be prohibited.

Opponents of the bid emphasised that the Government had listened to the fans and that the fans had had a tremendous impact and ensured that the 'inevitable' never happened. The war against Murdoch had been won!

Stephen Byers – Minister for Trade and Industry:

"The merger would damage the quality of British football."

Greg Dyke – Non-Executive Director, Manchester United, 1997-1999:

"Given my lifelong commitment to United, you can imagine how excited I was back in '96 when I was asked to join the Board of Manchester United.

Of course, I was on the Board of Manchester United when BSkyB tried to buy the company. I think it is well known that I was very much against the deal in principle and personally I was delighted when the Monopolies Commission came out against the takeover."

The War with Glazer:

Meanwhile, on the pitch Manchester United had been performing extraordinarily well. In a few amazing years they had won the fantastic treble. A League title, FA Cup victory and then victorious in the European Champions League Cup. A game won in dramatic fashion by coming back from a goal down and snatching victory with probably the last kicks of the game in time added on. The club went on to add more league titles to their trophy list.

But off the pitch a little-known American had been busy buying shares in Manchester United since early March 2003.

16th March 2003

The Takeover Panel assure Manchester United that Cubic Expression have no intention of making a bid for the club after they raised their stake in the club to 10.7%.

Glazer holds 2.9% below the level required to inform the Stock Exchange.

9th July 2003

The Cubic Expression increased their stake in the club to 11.4%.

14th September 2003

FANS UNITED IN DEFENCE OF UNITED

PRESS NOTICE:

For immediate release, 3.00pm, Sunday 14th September 2003. In response to yet more fevered speculation and hyperbole, surrounding the future ownership and stewardship of Manchester United plc, the club's independent supporter-shareholder organisation has warned that any potential suitors ignore the wishes and concerns of fans at their peril.

Oliver Houston – Shareholders United:

"Manchester United is not the plaything of wealthy individuals or international corporations. It is a 125-year-old community asset that should be run in the interests of its supporters. Anyone ignoring the 15 per cent, or so, of the shares held by fans is going to wind up with a bloody nose. Just ask Rupert Murdoch!
SU, IMUSA and the fanzines are united in the belief that no-one, other than the Supporters' Trust, should control 50 per cent or more of the Club."

26th September 2003

Malcolm Glazer had acquired 3.17%, taking his shareholding above the 3% threshold and, as required by legislation, he informed the club's management about it.

It wasn't long before rumours of a takeover began to circulate, though not specifically Glazer.

7th October 2003

Shares in Manchester United hit a new 2-year high after a mystery buyer bought 3 million shares. Rumours in the City thought Russian billionaire Boris Berezovsky might be trying to emulate Roman Abramovich.

The City was once again on full alert as Cubic Expression doubled their stake in Manchester United. The Irish pair bought BSkyB's 9.9% share in the club, taking their own stake to 23%.

BSkyB's decision to sell coincided with the high price of shares in Manchester United and helped the company to recoup some of the £60m they had invested in the club during the failed takeover in 1998.

Malcolm Glazer increased his shareholding to 9.66%, but repeatedly refused to comment on his share-buying.

Oliver Houston – Shareholders United:

"We don't need a sugar daddy."

29th November 2003

Glazer had increased his shareholding to 15% by November and he had had a meeting with the club's Chief Executive, David Gill, to discuss his intentions for the club. Gill described the Florida meeting.

David Gill – Chief Executive:

"Very friendly" and "useful and productive".

Football Club United of Manchester
Created from despair - Powered by passion

4th January 2004

Another Russian, Ralif Safin, one of the founders of Lukoil, is reported to be interested in buying Manchester United. There were doubts about his ability to raise the funds, but shares rose after accounts of his meeting a London Investment Bank were revealed.

12th February 2004

Glazer increased his shareholding to 16.31%.

The following day it was reported by *The Financial Times* that Glazer had instructed Commerzbank to explore a takeover bid. The club's value increased to £741.

15th February 2004

Magnier and McManus spent £20m and increase their shareholding to 29%. The shares belonged to Jon de Mol, the Dutch creator of the television show "Big Brother". He offered them enough shares to take them over the 30% line and which would oblige them to launch a full bid. The opportunity was declined and it is believed that the surplus shares went to Glazer.

Oliver Houston - Shareholders United:

"These guys have already shown that they are prepared to attack the club, the manager and its fans. What we appear to have seen is an attempt to take over the club without buying 100 per cent of the shares and fans will reject any notion of it. It is about time these guys stepped out of the shadows and told us exactly what they are trying to achieve."

16th February 2004

Manchester United placed in 'Offer Period' as Glazer makes an ambiguous statement claiming he is considering making an offer to buy the club.

24th February 2004

United are taken out of 'Offer Period' as Glazer makes another purchase.

29th February 2004

Malcolm Glazer spends £2.65m on another million Manchester United shares to increase his stake in the club to 16.69%.

Jules Spencer – Chairman of the Independent Manchester United Supporters' Association:

"The latest acquisition by Malcolm Glazer may be seen as a small investment by his standards, but it is another unwelcome one as far as we're concerned. Our message now is the same as it has always been. Manchester United is not for sale."

March 2004

Glazer states he has "no current intention" of buying Manchester United.

26th April 2004

Glazer buys another 4 million shares, taking his share to 18.25%. The shares previously belonged to Manchester United lawyer Maurice Watkins.

Football Club United of Manchester
Created from despair - Powered by passion

4th October 2004

Manchester United confirms to the Stock Exchange that they have received a 'Preliminary Approach'. The offer is traced back to Malcolm Glazer and the club goes back into the 'Offer Period'.

12th October 2004

In a Commons Motion, former Bury MP Alistair Burt, a staunch United fan, voiced his concern over Malcolm Glazer's takeover, stating that it could plunge Manchester United into debt. Mr Burt joined Chris Grayling, MP for Epsom and Ewell, in a protest campaign.

Malcolm Glazer had expressed an interest in buying the club the previous autumn and had tabled a motion which had been rejected by the club.

14th October 2004

Cubic Expression, the largest shareholders in Manchester United, admit to the Takeover Panel that they have broken off discussions with Malcolm Glazer.

15th October 2004

Glazer replies by launching an aggressive raid on the Stock Market, taking his stake to 25.3%.

Andy Walsh – Secretary, Independent Supporters Association:

"Malcolm Glazer has never been to Manchester and he is not wanted. We can only speculate about his motives, but we don't believe any of them will be of benefit, not just to our football club but to football as a whole. If he got his way, individual TV deals and a European Super League would be even closer to being realised. We will not let that happen."

18th October 2004
Glazer is in the market place again, raising his share to 27.63%.

19th October 2004
Once again Glazer raids the Stock Market and takes his share to 28.11% and finishes a five-day spending spree of £65m.

25th October 2004
The Manchester United Board break off negotiations with Glazer due to the large amount of money he would have to borrow in order to fulfil his quest. Manchester United is again taken out of the 'Offer Period'. Once again Glazer refuses to comment on the latest knock-back.

12th November 2004
Glazer tries to gain access to confidential files in Manchester United's books and fails.

As a major shareholder, Glazer carries out a threat and removes three directors from the Manchester United Board, Maurice Watkins, Philip Yea and Andy Anson, at the club's annual general meeting.

Manchester United releases a statement voicing their disappointment over Malcolm Glazer's actions and demand to know what his intentions for the club are.

Within 2 hours of the statement released by Manchester United, bankers JP Morgan and public relations company Brunswick inform Glazer that they are no longer interested in representing him.

Football Club United of Manchester
Created from despair - Powered by passion

21st November 2004

Sir Alex Ferguson – Manager:

"We don't want the club to be in anyone else's hands."

20th December 2004

Manchester United is again put in 'Offer Period' as they confirm Glazer has approached them with amendments to his original bid. Manchester United respond by telling Glazer that no further discussions will take place until Glazer has made a 'definitive proposal'.

1st February 2005

The Glazer family release a statement distancing themselves from reliable sources claiming that he was about to launch another bid for the club.

6th February 2005

Manchester United make it known that they have received a detailed proposal from Glazer which could lead to a bid.

9th February 2005

Manchester United fans stage a demonstration outside Old Trafford on Wednesday evening to protest against Glazer's plan to buy the club.

Tempers flare as 400+ fans chant "He's gonna die, Malcolm Glazer's gonna die, how we'll kill him I don't know, cut him up from head to toe". Supporters hang an effigy of the American from the gates of Old Trafford.

Fans ignore police requests to clear the streets and stage a sit-down protest.

The protests were aimed at Malcolm Glazer's latest attempt to buy the club after his previous efforts were rejected because of the high level of long-term debt the club would be saddled with.

Oliver Houston – Shareholders United:

"Our message to Manchester United is to close the book on Malcolm Glazer. He wants to know where the money is coming from within the club. Well, it comes from us, the fans.

If he takes over there won't be any coming in because we will not buy the merchandise, we will not go to the matches and United will not get the income they get now."

Mike – fan:

"I was there at most of the protests at OT. I wasn't involved at the centre of any of it; I was one of the crowd, although I think I stuck out a little bit because I always came straight from work and had my suit on.

I was there at the early stages of the night when the Glazers turned up at OT for the first time and the police set on the fans at the back of the ground. I helped to put a few things on the barricade at the front of the ground early on."

13th March 2005

Malcolm Glazer was not due to submit a revised takeover proposal for Manchester United before the end of the following week. The owner of the Tampa Bay Buccaneers American football team had hoped to get his 800 million pound revised business plan to United's board by the end of this week. Glazer still needs to meet with financial backers to finalise the debt package he will need to buy the world's richest soccer club. United's board had rejected two earlier bids from Glazer to buy the world's richest club.

28th April 2005

The Takeover Panel tell Glazer he has until 17th May to either make a bid or walk away.

29th April 2005

Shareholders United hatches plan:

Shareholders United (SU) sends a fax to all major shareholders in an amazing plan to thwart Glazer's takeover bid.

In an audacious £45m plot, SU hopes to buy a 6% block of shares and reach the required 10% that would prevent Glazer from reaching the compulsory purchase limit. The fax, whilst aimed at all shareholders, targeted Harry Dobson and his 6.5% share. It is thought that Cubic Expression would not be interested in selling.

SU:

"As you are aware, our aim is for the club to remain independent from ownership by any single person or company."

4th May 2005

The protests continued when a number of Manchester United fans' groups called for supporters to boycott the premiership match against West Bromwich Albion.

Apart from sending a message to Malcolm Glazer about his unwelcome attention, the fans' groups wanted to make David Gill aware that the fans would not tolerate obscene rises in ticket prices.

Jules Spencer – IMUSA Chairman:

"This is the last Saturday match-day opportunity for supporters to let any potential new owners and the current board know that supporters' loyalty can not be taken for granted. We realise it's asking a lot for people who have bought season tickets not to use them, but we feel we have to take a stand, not only on Glazer but also on the current board's obscene ticket price rises."

Shareholders United launches another audacious plan to stop Glazer, this time in the shape of a £100m package formed with preliminary backing of the Japanese investment Bank Nomura. The bank offered a pound-for-pound loan on cash pledged by the group to an investment trust. Shareholders United planned to contact all 7,000 fans who own in excess of 1,000 shares in the club. Once that motion is in process, it plans to raise funds by approaching celebrities and other wealthy fans and ask them to pledge money to the trust.

Nick Trowle – Shareholders United:

"I am confident because the numbers we need are relatively not that great. We have 2% of the shares under the SU umbrella already, so we are looking for another three or four per cent which equates to around £40m. This is a genuine attempt to safeguard the future of Manchester United."

7th May 2005

As the deadline looms for Glazer to make his bid for the club, Shareholders United claims a 300% increase in membership: from 8,682 in March 2004 to 25,876 a year later, with a fan base wide and diverse with celebrities ranking alongside Manchester United footballers and the ordinary fan.

Football Club United of Manchester
Created from despair - Powered by passion

Nick Trowle – Chairman, Shareholders United:

"This brilliant campaign, this amazing fight will go down in history – win or lose – and we will not lose."

12th May 2005

Despite protestations from MEC and other supporters' groups, Glazer reaches an agreement with Magnier and McManus to buy their 28.7% share, giving him the controlling stake with around 57%. He then manages to secure the stake of Scottish mining entrepreneur Harry Dobson, taking his share to 62% and finally, hours later, he buys another 9.8%, taking his total to 71.8%.

Glazer now launches his £790.3m takeover of Manchester United in a move that catches the Manchester United directors by surprise. It had been anticipated that Glazer would launch a formal takeover bid to all the shareholders before obtaining the agreement of McManus and Magnier.

Mark Longden – Independent Manchester United Supporters Association:

"They have sold the Manchester United heritage. They have proved that they were never interested in Manchester United or football."

More than 50 angry Manchester United fans stormed a function at the Manchester Art Gallery. JP Morgan was in Manchester for the National Association for Pensions Conference and was holding a drinks reception for their clients. Wine was thrown but no damage done to the artwork.

In other incidents, disgruntled fans raided the offices of Rothschild the investment bank and pizza was sent every hour to the offices of Brunswick the P.R. company which used to represent Glazer.

Oliver Houston – Shareholders United:

"This is by no means over. Manchester United is going to become an extremely tainted brand. People will feel that this is no longer their club."

Mark Longden – Independent Manchester United Supporters Association:

"They [Magnier and McManus] have sold the Manchester United heritage. They have proved that they were never interested in Manchester United or football."

Ted Fellows (fan): "This is terrible news. I thought it would have been avoided with all that has been happening with Shareholders United and the protests that have been going on recently. This is a dark day for Manchester United."

Politico – fan:

"12th May, 3.50pm.

I was just about to duck under the water in my bath.

Then the words I had been fearing for several weeks came on the Simon Mayo show on 5 Live: 'Magnier and McManus have sold their shares to Malcolm Glazer'.

"FUCK!" was all I could say as I jumped out of the bath – I had to do something, so I chucked on the nearest clothes I could find.

As I half fell and half ran down the stairs and burst into the kitchen I shouted to my somewhat bemused better half, 'the bastard's done it, he's got control, we're finished.'

Football Club United of Manchester
Created from despair - Powered by passion

I quickly said I had got to go to OT straight away, and seeing how upset I was Cheryl knew this was not a time to argue.

I asked where my flag was. Why, I was asked. Because that's it, MUFC are dead; so I am going to burn my flag live on telly.

Cheryl was not happy – this was no shop-bought piece of printed nylon, but one carefully sewn together by my wife to celebrate our first Premiership in 1992.

She pleaded with me not to do it, but I needed to symbolise what I could only rationalise as a death in the family – and destroying the flag was as good a way as anything.

The 40-minute drive to OT passed in a blur; my only thoughts being, how can everyone just carry on with their everyday lives when that 'orrible bastard had got his claws into United and would instantly turn it from the planet's most profitable football club into the most debt-laden.

I parked where I always had – just over the bridge from Warwick Road station – and walked past the cricket ground. Immediately I could hear noise up ahead and pretty soon it became clear that several hundred fans were sitting down, stopping the traffic on the very busy Chester Road.

This is where I turned into an apprentice media whore – and failed.

TV cameras and reporters were covering what was already a pretty vociferous demo, so I approached the reporter and said I wanted to burn my flag on camera, which he agreed to do.

One technical hitch, cos my missus was too clever. Neither would the flag burn as it was flame-retardant material, nor did it even rip up very easily – but, regardless, I got to spout off for a minute live on Sky and got my point across OK.

We decided to march down to the ground next and prevented

scores of people from gaining access to corporate dining for 30 minutes or so until the good old GMP got themselves organised.

I did my best to wind up the officer in front of me, asking him politely why it was against the law to shout 'SCUM SCUM SCUM' at the people going in to the North Stand.

He leaned forward and whispered a less than subtle warning – so at that I started in an exaggerated manner looking for his number. He was on the edge, and I was about to get on a plane to Canada the next day, so getting nicked was not going to go down well domestically.

I also tried to rationalise that they were just doing their job, but all we were doing was shouting and chanting: not exactly major public disorder, but we were kicking back against the system and at that precise moment that is exactly what the police represented.

How could it possibly be fair what was happening.

Reluctantly, I made my way home simply feeling numb."

Tommy Docherty – Manager, 1972-77:

"The man has almost bought the club, and he knows nothing about football.

I think he will recoup his money as quick as he possibly can, no matter who it involves, and no matter who it hurts. Manchester United's heart and soul has been sold today. It has changed for ever today."

Dean – fan:

"On the day I was in college and I had just came back in from lunch to meet my tutor, and as I was waiting I got a text off my mate saying it had happened. I didn't believe it at first, so I was straight onto Red Issue and luckily just got on it and had a quick scan around to see it was true, and then it crashed; so I went over to BBC and saw it on the ticker. I just couldn't believe. I didn't think it would happen as I believed that 'Coolmore' would keep to their word and not sell out and I also believed some of the rumours that Shareholders United had near 20%. I still thought we had a chance to get a 25% stake and keep him out. I was thinking that I had been to my last ever United game (vs. Chelsea) and remembering how it felt at the end of that game with the lap of honour and the atmosphere in the ground, so weird. I joined in with the badgering of the banks, I sent a load of black page faxes to the bank and signed all their e-mails up for everything I could, as well as sending my own e-mails explaining that I felt what they were doing was wrong, in a more aggressive tone. I also pledged all the money I could into shares through SU, which didn't amount to much, to be fair. I was pestering everyone I knew for a tenner just so I could sign them up, but that didn't really work."

13th May 2005

'Cold Feet' actor James Nesbitt was requested to do voiceover commercial for Manchester United to promote their new Quadrant boxes. As a life-long 'Red', he jumped at the chance; but soon after he realised that Manchester United fans felt betrayed by his actions. He generously donated half of his fee to Shareholders United with the other half going to UNICEF.

Christopher Eccleston, or 'Doctor Who' to his followers, had already donated £10,000 to Shareholders United.

Nick Towle – Shareholders United:

"Glazer will soon realise, if he doesn't know it already, that we will not be going away quietly. These are massive debts; where is the extra revenue coming from? This will put huge pressure on United to perform, both on and off the pitch. Some estimates believe that an extra 50 to 70 million pounds will be needed to service the debts."

14th May 2005

Manchester United fans now know that Red Football, the title of Glazer's bid, will receive £275m funding from preferred securities which have not been secured against the club's assets and £265m that will. Given that United's most recent half-yearly profits were £12.4m, it is clear that the new owner will have to manufacture an extremely substantial increase in turnover in order to pay the debt.

Considering that there have not been any details released from Glazer's business plan in a deal Gill describes as 'aggressive', leads supporters to believe that there will be increases in ticket prices and an attempt to scrap current Premier League collective bargaining agreement.

Nick Towle – Shareholders United:

"These massive debts have to be serviced, both interest payments and repayment of the principal, and it seems that the revenues of Manchester United will be the prime source of that servicing requirement."

15th May 2005

Reports that Manchester United fans are planning to disrupt the

FA Cup Final as part of the campaign to stop Glazer taking over the club. Possible ploys include successive pitch invasions; another is throwing thousands of beach balls onto the pitch or staging a sit-down protest on the turf.

Oliver Houston – Vice-Chairman, Shareholders United:

"We won't do anything that endangers safety but they have to draft in the army to police the match."

FA Spokesperson:

"We are looking forward to a wonderful event on Saturday."

16th May 2005

A milestone for Glazer as he reached the 75% stake in the club that allowed him to delist the club from the London Stock Exchange and he expressed his desire to do so within 20 days.

17th May 2005

D-Day for Glazer. The Takeover Panel had decided Malcolm Glazer had until today to either 'put up or shut up' on his takeover of the club.

26th May 2005

The Manchester United Board tells its shareholders to accept Malcolm Glazer's price of £3 per share.

Nick Towle – Chairman, Shareholders United:

"We hope Malcolm Glazer's stay is as short as possible, and over the coming seasons we will pursue a twin-track strategy to reclaim United."

7th June 2005

Glazer appointed his sons Joel, Avram and Bryan to the Plc Board of Manchester United as non-executive directors. Sir Roy Gardner resigned his position as Chairman of the Plc Board along with non-executive directors Jim O'Neill and Ian Much.

10th June 2005

Documents seen by a newspaper reveal Glazer's business plans for the club. This includes aggressive measures to triple the club's profits, which include raising ticket prices by 54% by 2010 and limiting transfer funds to £25m per year. Glazer also anticipates a boost of 76% in the commercial turnover of the club, driven by increased sales to the fans.

"The drive for commercialism is becoming too much for most fans," said Nick Trowle. "It's really beginning to create a big problem, and that's just before fans stop buying the products and merchandise, which will also increase in price. Our campaign is to urge fans to exercise their consumer choice and just not buy the products of the club or the products of the company and the products of the sponsors."

After threats were made against David Gill, the Chief Executive of the club, who many fans feel did not do enough to repel Glazer, Greater Manchester Police said they were taking the threats seriously.

Police Chief:

"All reports will be investigated thoroughly."

Joel Glazer told BBC radio:

"Things are still up in the air. Plans have not been finalised.

Nothing has been signed off. These are speculative numbers." Rumours that Sir Bobby Charlton would be dismissed from the Board were also refuted.

14th June 2005

With his percentage now 97.3, he had enough shares to assume complete control over the club and with it the option to force the remainder of shareholders to sell their shares to him.

Nick Towle – Chairman of Shareholders United:

"I'm not so sure it has. He certainly gets control of the club and will end up with more than 90%; that is my guess. We will wait and see how far he gets, but there are things we can do by law to make life difficult for him and a lot of Manchester United fans want to do that."

22nd June 2005

Glazer delists the club from the London Stock Exchange.

28th June 2005

Glazer finally achieves the 98% necessary to gain a compulsory order for the remainder of the shares and the club's final valuation is $1.47b.

The £3 per share offer is to remain open for the foreseeable future for the remaining 2% of shareholders.

23rd November 2005

Vodafone prematurely ended its £36m four-year shirt sponsorship with the club.

The deal still had one year left to run, but they chose to

terminate the agreement early in order to concentrate on Champions League football, said a Vodafone spokesman.

Manchester United Supporters Trust (MUST) had urged Vodafone to end its relationship with Manchester United as the brand had become 'tainted'.

12th February 2006
Greg Dyke – Non-Executive Director (Man Utd), 1997-1999:

"When you think about United and Brentford there is an irony. United became a public company, and part of the supposed benefit was that fans could own some shares. Now it's owned by a bunch of Americans who don't give a toss about Manchester or British football. They know nothing about it, and put it in hock. Brentford is now owned by the fans, and actually I've come to the conclusion that that's the best thing for a football club. United's is a sad story. It had no debt and built that whole magnificent ground from current cash flow. Now it's got £600m of debt. They [the Glazers] were the wrong people to buy the club. It was a terrible decision."

18th June 2006

Three more members of the Glazer family join the Board at Manchester United.

Sons Kevin and Edward and daughter Darcie join the club as non-executive directors.

Chapter 2: Meetings

May 2005

Approximately 2,000 desperate fans attend an emergency meeting in the Apollo Theatre, arranged for the May Bank Holiday. The meeting was set up by the 'Not for Sale' Coalition who were opposed to the Malcolm Glazer takeover. Glazer had reached 75% of the shares in the club the month before and the meeting of the Red fans was in part anti-Glazer and in part anti-corporate.

These meetings where the wearing of the red uniform bonded the fans together were an exception. The 'uniform' was not worn.

"As long as our club is owned by Glazer, I'm not wearing any official kit," vowed a young speaker to cheers of support.

Kris Stewart, the Chairman of AFC Wimbledon, had attended meetings of angry fans – fans so strongly opposed to Glazer and his takeover that they would've done anything to stop him and anyone else who had the nerve. The support appeared vocal enough and it was felt that 1,000 pledges would be enough to ensure that the birth of the team would be creditable.

When the pledges failed to materialise, many hundreds of fans were deflated. Months of protesting not just at Old Trafford but at the offices of the investment bankers and sponsors of Manchester United. Buying of shares, sending faxes, e-mails, phone calls, meetings rallying the troops together, took its toll. The sheer drain on people was enormous and to gather everything together in order to get the new club up and running with a business plan, website, letterheads, management, name, strip, badge, a ground to play at, all seemed impossible.

Kris Stewart had made one impassioned speech to the fans and he raised his voice one more time. "Why do you need 1,000 pledges anyway? Do you really believe that the support is out there?" he questioned the masses. The answer was "yes". "Well, go for it then," he urged.

The weary abject muttering hushed and was replaced by a positive stirring of approval, the grindings of a massive power gathering its energy and speed began. Suddenly, instead of not having a team or ground or anywhere to play, voices from the darkness volunteered their services. With 16 days to go before an application had to go to the County FA, time was short; 9 people began to share the tasks, then 7 more joined in as more work was generated. The club's name, pledges needed sorting, votes on badges, strips, kit suppliers sourced, the task appeared insurmountable; but finally a creditable application was made to the County FA. All of the preliminary hard work paid off when the club was elected to join the league.

Outside the theatre, many fans were taking advantage of the Nike amnesty and handing in their replica strips and trainers to charity. Boycotting the official merchandise is part of the gameplan employed by the anti-takeover campaign and putting pressure on Nike as one of the major suppliers to Manchester United by not buying its equipment.

Many fans didn't renew their season tickets in protest at Glazer's hostile takeover, whilst others who couldn't make the ultimate sacrifice planned to do their bit by eschewing the traditional half-time refreshments and reminding others who do not to!

Football Club United of Manchester

Created from despair - Powered by passion

Andy Walsh – Chairman of the coalition:

"People are getting a harsh exposure to what football has become!"

Fans keen to take direct action urged a campaign of stink bombs on the terraces whilst a female member suggested a topless invasion, a suggestion met by the kind of cheering normally reserved for the injury-time winner in a cup final!

Chapter 3: A New Club

The idea of forming a new football club had been mooted during the fight against Rupert Murdoch when he tried unsuccessfully to take over Manchester United. The idea of a new club was thought to be too radical. The formation of the club took on more credibility during the fight with Malcolm Glazer, and although the supporters had their own reasons for wanting the new club, Glazer's unwanted takeover was the catalyst behind it. The new club was formed in the summer of 2005.

During a Manchester United supporters' meeting on 19th May 2005, Andy Walsh, the chairman, announced that a second meeting would be taking place on 30th May at the Apollo Theatre to discuss further the new club. It was also announced that Kris Stewart, the chairman of AFC Wimbledon, had given advice on forming a new club. AFC Wimbledon is another supporter-owned club. Stewart was to address a subsequent meeting and offered AFC Wimbledon's support.

The club 'FC United of Manchester' was registered as a bona fide football club with Manchester County Football Association on 14th June 2005 and was accepted into the North West Counties League in the same month. There were four spaces available in the division and so no teams were rejected because of FC United's application. The North West Counties Football League is on level 10 in the English football league system, 9 levels lower than the English Premier League.

Football Club United of Manchester
Created from despair - Powered by passion

Scott Holt – player:

"Over the summer I heard about FC United from a good mate, Darren Lyons. I attended pre-season training and played in the first ever friendly against Leigh RMI. It was an amazing experience. We got changed and a few fans were there, not many, and we started doing the warm-up. I'd played in front of small crowds before, so wasn't phased. Then the ground was gradually filling. When we came out for kick-off, a lad asked for my autograph and I looked around and the ground was pretty much full. The noise was frightening and I remember thinking these are here to watch us. It was like nothing I had experienced before. I knew it was serious when we travelled down the night before and people were coming into the hotel asking for pictures and the next day 1000's of fans were singing songs for 90 minutes. FC United fans were outnumbered by the AFC Wimbledon fans, but they were outsung by the FC United fans.

Then, when I returned to work, a colleague put an article from the *Guardian* on my desk with a picture of me in the dressing room at AFC Wimbledon. It was a great feeling and a great thing to be a part of."

Wolfie – fan:

"I was vehemently opposed to Glazer on principle rather than from a business point of view, just as I was opposed to Murdoch or indeed anyone else who thought they could just walk into town and buy my team. However, I'd been fairly peripheral at Old Trafford for a couple of years for a number of reasons (money, growing older, not enjoying it any more, just not feeling I was particularly welcome) and, whilst I supported all the anti-Glazer groups and protests, I just had a feeling that it would all turn out right and Glazer would be shown the door. When a work colleague told me about the concept of FC United, I pointed out it would be no better than me forming my own team ... the North West could be full of mini-Uniteds ... it was, I concluded, a daft idea.

I was in Skipton on the day it finally happened, visiting an old friend. A Leeds fan in the pub thought it was the best thing ever."

Club Manifesto:

FC United of Manchester is a new football club founded by disaffected and disenfranchised Manchester United supporters. Our aim is to create a sustainable club for the long term which is owned and democratically run by its members, which is accessible to all the communities of Manchester and one in which they can participate fully. Although driven by very different circumstances, FC United of Manchester takes as its inspiration a number of supporters' groups who have gone down this route, including AFC Wimbledon, who have offered unstinting support.

FC United of Manchester is intended to create a football club which addresses the concerns which many Manchester United fans have had over the last decade or more with how the club and football have developed, culminating in the club's takeover by Malcolm Glazer. We will follow the best traditions of Manchester United's past by developing policies which encourage youth participation in terms of both playing and supporting.

FC United of Manchester will be formed as a member-owned, democratic, and non-profit-making entity on the Industrial and Provident Society company model. The EGM will focus on the election of a board of directors by the members, and the direction of the club over the coming season.

We have ambitious and long-term plans. Above all, we want to be seen as a good example of how a club can be run in the interests of its members and be of benefit to its local communities. However, we are a new club and will require patience in order to reach our goals. With the help of all our members and supporters we are confident we can achieve them.

Seven core principles of how the club will operate are set out below, and once agreed by the membership, will be protected by all elected Board members:

- The Board will be democratically elected by its members.
- Decisions taken by the membership will be decided on a one member, one vote basis.
- The club will develop strong links with the local community and strive to be accessible to all, discriminating against none.
- The club will endeavour to make admission prices as affordable as possible, to as wide a constituency as possible.
- The club will encourage young, local participation – playing and supporting – whenever possible.
- The Board will strive wherever possible to avoid outright commercialism.
- The club will remain a non-profit organisation.

Chapter 4: FCUoM's friendly debut

On a day when the sun could only shine, thousands of man hours came together in one big celebration. All the time, effort and money pitched against Glazer's takeover left many reeling in the gutter and with weary bodies bowed, but not broken, they created a team.

Out of the dazzling sunlight came FC United of Manchester, proud and strong.

More than 2,500 fans turned up at the home of Leigh RMI to see history being made. One complete end of Hilton Park was packed with FC United supporters doing what they do best, singing. When the team took to the field the fans announced their arrival to the world with a tumultuous roar – FC United had arrived! The game ended in a 0-0 draw with Barrie George producing some stunning saves in goal, Kevin Elvin, Gareth Ormes and Rob Nugent holding firm in defence. Joz Mitten, Scott Holt and Steve Torpey caused problems for their defence and the draw was well earned.

16th July 2005. K.O. 15.00.

Leigh RMI vs FC United of Manchester

Teams:

Leigh RMI

Lamb, Hughes, Dibble, Dunne, Coyne, Smith, Ellison, Brockley, Howarth, Roscoe, Drew, Peyton, Stoker, S Smith, Tench, Taylor, Girdlestone, Galloway, McDiamond, Shillito, McDowell, McDonnagh, Ashmole, Morton, Thompson.

Football Club United of Manchester

Created from despair - Powered by passion

FC United

Priestley, George, Elvin, McCartney, Nugent, Gilligan, P Mitten, Coyne, Rawlinson, Hevicon, Torpey, J Mitten, Orr, Fleury, Ormes, Holt, Hayley, Trees, Weston, Lyons, Power.

Wolfie – fan:

"The same colleague who initially drew my attention to FCUoM kept me updated as to the progress ... the trials, the badge, the date of the first friendly ... his enthusiasm proved so effective I was the one who ended up looking at bus times to Leigh, and I roped a couple more friends in too.

When we arrived at Leigh that sunny Saturday, the first pub we came to was bursting with Reds ... there were people in there that we knew but we hadn't known were going. The atmosphere was like a United away match, something I'd not experienced for a while, with the whole pub singing. We had a great day at the match, and the common consensus was when we would do it again.

There were a few more of us for our next journey out to Stalybridge, and it was here we heard 'Under The Boardwalk' being sung for the first time. Days out at the football like this had seemed to be a thing of the past for me – not getting on trains because they were too full, meeting new people and sharing taxis from the pub, singing new songs, being in strange towns after a match."

Dom – fan:

"The first game at Leigh, I didn't know what to think; a mixture of emotions, everything had moved so quickly, which was important if the whole idea was to get off the ground. Either way, I headed down to Leigh on my own, as the friend of mine who came along to the protests with me didn't think it was such a good idea; but I went with an open mind and gave it a chance. This is something I'm extremely glad I'd done, because, from that day forward, I became encapsulated in a football revolution, following FCUoM up and down the country, making new friends, enjoying watching football on the terraces, singing along, having fun. The emotion at the end of the Leigh game, on the pitch with the players, was something I'd never experienced before; it was different, something special."

Joz Mitten – player:
"It was brilliant to be able to play in front of a crowd that big. All the players got a big buzz from it."

Chapter 5: FCUoM's Pre-season friendlies

Once the club had been formed it was important to gain match fitness and pre-season friendlies are a must. Due to the hype surrounding FC United, there were no shortage of takers and Leigh RMI, Stalybridge, Flixton, as well as some fixtures not published, were all made use of to gain experience and match fitness. It was also a good time for the new manager to try out players without all the fuss that might or might not go with them.

Both Karl Marginson the manager and Phil Power the assistant manager had played with Stalybridge Celtic during their playing careers and as Myra Mandryk, a popular figure at Stalybridge, required medical treatment, FC United offered to play against them in a trophy match. 30th July 2005 saw a hard fought match played in front of 2,000 screaming fans that FC United lost 2-0 and so the second chance of winning silverware went begging.

Teams:

Stalybridge Celtic

Pettinger, Smith, Barnard, Keeling, Haran, Wharton, S Smith, Price, Ellington, Turley, Prince, Mulvaney, Black, Buxton, Eastwood, Murcott.

FC United

Priestley, Elvin, Nugent, Ormes, Rawlinson, Coyne (Capt), Spencer, Patterson, Torpey, Fleury, Orr, J Mitten, Hevicon, P Mitten, Holt, Hayley.

Politico – fan:

"Within 3 months, incredibly, I would be standing on the terraces watching FC United of Manchester at Stalybridge Celtic, the club I had contributed towards in a pre-season friendly. A guy stood next to me and, beaming as we launched into a bizarre version of 'Under the Boardwalk', said, 'This is better than Milan   away.'

How right he was and the biggest silver lining had been found on the darkest of clouds."

Chapter 6: Supporters Direct Cup

Kris Stewart, Chairman of AFC Wimbledon, knew all about club beginnings, having been involved with one. He was invited up to Manchester to speak at the meetings concerning the creation of the new club.

"I've always been an ABU (Anyone but United) fan and was delighted when they lost the FA Cup in 1976. But those people connected to FC United, those I met in Manchester and those I've spoken to since, are good people. They're the decent football fans who have become more and more disillusioned over time with the way the game has been changing, and want to get back to following a genuine football club."

The game challenging for the Supporters Direct Cup is between clubs who are fan-driven and was won by AFC Wimbledon 1-0. The hard-fought game played in brilliant sunshine watched by 3,301 cheering fans was lost by a single goal by AFC Wimbledon's Ricci Crace, with FC United shot-stopper Barrie George voted man of the match.

Teams:

AFC Wimbledon

Little, Wojciechowski, Sargent, Howard, Butler, Sobihy, York, Moore, R Butler, Smeltz, Woolner, Cooper, Lennie, Judge, Crace, Kouman, Gray, Campbell, Bates, Hillier, McDowall.

FC United

George, Tree, Ormes, Rawlinson (Capt), Nugent, Elvin, Hayley,

Coyne, J Mitten, Torpey, Orr, Lyons, Priestly, Gilligan, Weston, Hevingham, Jean, Holt, Power.

A

Abandoned Games: Even though FC United are ground-sharing with Bury FC and the ground is used on a regular basis, there were no abandoned games during the 2005/6 or 2006/7 seasons.

Acceptance: Football Club United of Manchester (FCUoM) applied to join the North West Counties Football League for the season 2005-06 and were accepted on 18th June 2005.

Admission: The majority of tickets sold at grounds for matches at this level cost around £6 or £7, and £2 or £4 for concessions. However, FCUoM broke with tradition and for the match against Blackpool Mechanics on 10th September 2005 allowed free access for under 18s. Those under 18 season ticket holders were presented with a free pin badge as recognition of their commitment to the club. The reason: to make live football more accessible to youngsters. Over 700 fans took up the generous offer.

The same offer was made for the quarter-final home game against Nelson.

Football Club United of Manchester
Created from despair - Powered by passion

AFC Wimbledon: In the summer of 2002, the FA Commission granted permission for a group of businessmen to move the local football team some 70 miles away from its natural home and devoted fan base. After the initial shock and dismay, the fans saw another opportunity: the chance to create their own team. Backed by the Wimbledon Independent Supporters Association (WISA) and the Dons Trust, AFC Wimbledon was born. Six weeks later, with a ground, senior status, acceptance into the Combined Counties League and a couple of hundred season ticket applications, AFC Wimbledon played its first friendly against Sutton United in front of 4,500 fans. AFC Wimbledon amassed 111 points, but early inconsistency cost them promotion in their inaugural season; but the 2003/04 season told a different story and AFC Dons were promoted. An impressive record of 42 wins, 4 draws, no losses, with 130 points and a goal difference of +148, saw them win the title. The season was completed when they won the Premier Challenge Cup, finishing a league and cup double. The summer of 2004 saw the Dons back in the Isthmian League for the first time since 1964.

Ahern, William (Midfielder): Born 4/2/1987 in Islington, North London.

Will Ahern proved to be a hidden diamond when his talents were spotted by his school teacher. Will didn't consider playing football as a career when he took part in playground kick-abouts. He avoided joining clubs when his mates were being selected; instead, he focused on his school team, where he was used as a striker or winger. His favourite position is central midfield and it was there he played when he helped his school team St Anne's to win the Trafford School Trophy.

Things took a turn when he moved to high school: the pace was faster and more competitive, but he still rejected joining any clubs and it wasn't until his teacher suggested he try for the Borough Schoolboy trials that he began to realise his ambitions. He was selected from the hundreds of enthusiastic triallists and played for Trafford Schoolboys. The more football he played the more his talents became obvious and the manager pointed him out to a friend at Macclesfield Town, who took him for a trial.

William quickly impressed and he was offered a place on schoolboy terms and he was fortunate enough to break into the 1st team, but it was an unfortunate injury that sidelined him when it was time for the YTS placements to be handed out and he was released.

He left school and the club disillusioned and tried out with Urmston Town and Old Stretfordians, but to no avail.

Eventually he found someone who believed in his talents and he was asked to join Newcastle Town. With his football back on track, he gained a place on an apprenticeship on a plastering course and Will's confidence began to rise.

Will had heard of FC United and, despite being at Newcastle Town, he headed for the friendly game against Flixton in September 2005 and played in front of 1,500 screaming fans.

Will earned himself a place in the squad and made an impressive start to his FC United career from the subs bench, only to be struck down by an injury which kept him out of the side until November, returning in the League Challenge Cup game with Darwen FC.

He made his full debut the following week against New Mills, where he forged a midfield partnership with Simon Carden that saw the club go on a 10-match unbeaten run, making it impossible for the manager to split the pair. Will is the youngest player to appear for FCUoM and scored his first goal for the club on 18/2/2006 against Blackpool Mechanics. Despite his tender years, he was the first player to have a trial with a league club. Grimsby Town took him on trial in March 2005 but fortunately for FC United they didn't sign him.

He became the first player to be sent off in the 2006/7 season when red carded against Curzon Ashton in the September.

William left the club in December 2006 with the club's blessing to go travelling.

Allen, Danny (Forward): Born 18/1/1988 in Stockport.

Reserve Squad.

Having a father who ran a soccer school and coached football and a soccer-mad family, it was inevitable that Danny would catch the football bug.

Danny joined Boundary Park as an 8-year-old and played on the wing or as a glory-hunting striker and soon joined Cheadle. Danny's speed, fleet of foot and goal-scoring ability brought him to the attention of Oldham and he was invited to a 6-week trial. He performed sufficiently well enough to be offered schoolboy terms.

Playing so close to Oldham Athletic FC was a bonus, as there was a greater chance of being seen by the local coaches and it came as no surprise that Danny had his high school education cut short by the offer of a Youth Training Scheme (YTS) place at Oldham.

It wasn't long before his extraordinary talent attracted the bigger clubs and it wasn't long before he was offered trials at both Manchester clubs and he spent time with youth sides. Manchester City was the first to offer a concrete contract, so he signed, despite being a huge Manchester United fan.

Having secured a football contract, Danny began to concentrate more on football than education and, as unfortunately happens to many youngsters, Danny was struck down by a serious knee injury and spent the first few months sitting on the sidelines while the others progressed. By the time Danny regained fitness, it was apparent who was going to be offered a contract and who wasn't. The young Danny left Manchester City and almost gave up on football, but his desire to make it as a professional footballer won through and he joined Chadderton FC. His fitness levels were higher than most and there was certainly less pressure to perform and Danny began to enjoy his football again. He even enrolled into a football college where he could study football, play football, as well as the other aspects of football such as diet and fitness.

While Danny spent the next two years studying for his diploma, he also had to endure two years of listening to FC United reserve player Ryan Shaughnessy singing the praises of the newly-formed club. Curiosity finally got the better of him and he had trials with FC United at the beginning of the 2006/7 season, unfortunately not making the youth side but making the reserve side instead.

It wasn't long before Danny's prolific scoring caught the eye of the manager. He earned himself a place on the subs bench and, coming on against Glossop North End in a game that had been effectively won, there was no pressure on him to score until the FA Vase cup game against Salford City in November 2006, which ended in a hard fought 3-2 victory. Danny came on as a substitute in the second half and after the game he went on to play for the Reserves against Flixton in the Reserves Cup on the same day.

Danny made his first start against Stone Dominos in the November 2006 and, on a day where every move, every ball and every shot all came off, he scored a hat trick in the 7-0 win.

Altrincham FC: Altrincham FC has strong ties to FC United as initially 11 former players have found their way to FC United: shot-stopper Barry George, triallists Mark Rawlinson and Ryan Gilligan, Steve Torpey, Rob Trees, Joz Mitten, Aaron Hevingham, Ryan Hevicon, Darren Lyons, goal machine Adie Orr and young Phil Power.

Anti-Racism: To respect the Anti-Racism Week, FCUoM played their part by having the players carrying out a banner reading "FC United Against Racism" before the home game against Nelson on 22/10/05.

Appearances, Least: The record for the least number of league appearances belongs to Phil Priestly, who appeared in just one league game against Winsford Town. Ryan Hevicon and Rob Trees made just one appearance in pre-season friendlies before moving on.

This refers to players who have since left the club and doesn't take into account players who are current but have yet to play for FCUoM.

Most: In the first season the record for the most appearances is thirty-three by the right back Steve Spencer, playing in 30 league games and 3 cup games.

Sam Ashton bettered this in the 2006/7 season by making 40 league and 10 cup game appearances.

Ashton, Samuel Seth (Goalkeeper): Born 9/10/1986 in Bolton.

Sam was born into a football family and it wasn't too long before he caught the bug himself and was captain of his school team and an excellent striker.

It was when Sam joined Oxford Lads Club he went in goal, but it was his goal-scoring ability that got him noticed and the 9-year-old went down to Bolton Wanderers for a trial. Unfortunately, the goalkeeper broke his arm and Sam went in goal and performed heroics. Alas, it wasn't to be and nothing came of it. It wasn't for another two years that Sam caught the attention of Bolton Wanderers again and he was invited down for a second trial. This time, however, his skill shone through and he was offered schoolboy terms. Sam was delighted to accept and went as far as to have a Bolton Wanderers tattoo!

Sam progressed at Bolton, broke into the second XI and played for the reserves against Birmingham in a 2-2 draw.

Leaving school and playing football is everyone's dream and Sam was no exception. Initially, it went well, but in the second year

Sam injured his finger, which kept him side-lined for 3 months and while he fought to maintain his fitness Bolton bought in two new keepers. Sam continued to play to the best of his abilities and in a bizarre twist the goalie was named as a substitute in the 3rd round FA Cup game against Watford in January 2006. Sam had played outfield in a training session against the first team and had managed to contain the first team striker Stelios to such an extent that the manager, Big Sam Allardyce, had Sam train as an outfield player and with 5 minutes to go he was sent on to play as an outfield player! Unfortunately, he was released shortly afterwards and he had trials with Rochdale, Cambridge United and Radcliffe Borough. Sam was listed in the squad to play against FC United in a pre-season friendly in the July and it was the Radcliffe manager that put Sam in touch with Karl Marginson, and in July 2006 he made his debut for FC United in the friendly against Bury and went on to make his competitive debut for the club in the first league game of the season against St Helens Town, keeping a clean sheet in the 2-0 win. Sam made 50 league and cup appearances in his first season with the club.

Assistant Manager: The current assistant manager is Phil Power.

Attendance, Highest: Even though the 'United United' day had 3,808 fans in attendance due to 'Big United' not having a home game that day and the Man United supporters being invited down to Gigg Lane to see 'Little United' play. The second highest home attendance was 4,328 on 2nd January 2006, when FCUoM were at home to Winsford FC in what the fans lovingly called 'Big Coat

Day'. Many doubters believed that once FC United had been formed and the honeymoon period was over, that on cold, wet, miserable days the fans would stay away and when one fan was asked what he would do on such days he replied, "I'll wear my big coat then!" Apart from wanting to prove the doubters wrong, this fixture against Winsford was first versus second and valuable points were at stake. FC United won 2-1, fighting back from a goal down.

The record attendance for a home game was 6,023 for the last home game of the season on 22nd April 2006, when FC United were presented with the Division Two Trophy and promoted as champions.

The highest away attendance was 4,300 at Bloomfield Road, home of Blackpool FC. Blackpool Mechanics changed the venue for their home game on 18th February 2006. FC United won 4-2.

The 23-year-old NWCFL attendance record had already been broken by FC United on the first day of the season, when 2,590 fans turned up at Harrison Park to watch the 5-2 away win over Leek CSOB.

FC United were the second-best supported team in non-league football in 2005/6, with an average gate of 3,056, behind Exeter City and above their League Two hosts Bury.

The highest attendance for the 2006/7 season was 3,381 for the home game against Silsden in September 2006.

4,058 turned out for the away fixture against Salford City in October 2006.

Lowest: The lowest attendance figure at a home league game was 1,978 at home to Eccleshall on 24th August 2005. The lowest attendance for an away fixture was 1,028 on 27th February 2006 against Great Harwood Town.

FCUoM took advantage of a Saturday off to play a game behind locked doors at the Thorn Cross Young Offenders Institution, where spectators were, understandably, not invited. FCUoM won 7-1.

The lowest away attendance in the 2006/07 season was against Nelson, when 640 fans turned out to see the 8-0 win on 4th April 2007.

On 13th September 2006, 1,566 supporters saw the home game with Abbey Hey and enjoyed the 7-1 victory.

Auction: Various items, mainly programmes, have appeared on the auction site E-bay. Programmes have had as high a price as £22.50, although one autographed programme had an asking price of £45.00. Other items for sale have included badges, DVDs, videos, flags and scarves.

Average: FC United's average gate was 3,059 and the club were 92nd in an attendance league of over 900 teams, including Premiership, Championship and league sides, in their first season 2005/6.

For the 2006/7 season, FC United's average gate was 4,090.

Awards: FC United were voted the 'Club of the Year 2005/6'. The award was presented by ex-Manchester United star Sammy McIlroy. The Step 6 award from the Non-League Paper is an annual award and covers the whole national non-league scene. Rory Patterson received the Step 6 'Player of the Year' award for 2005/6.

FC United also collected the 'Programme of the Season' award.

FC United won 'Newcomer of the Year' award in the prestigious BBC North West Sports Awards 2006. Karl Darren and Phil collected the award from the boxer Amir Khan.

Rory Patterson was also voted 'Young Player of the Year' in football's non-league newspaper for the season 2006/7.

Away Wins: FC United won away from home 13 times in their first season, a feat bettered in the second season by winning 17 games away from home.

B

Badges: A number of well thought out and designed badges were put forward to be the crest of FCUoM. Three were rejected after careful consideration. A vote was taken in July at the EGM for the club badge, with the winning design by Matt Wilkinson chosen from a list of three. His design achieved over 50% of the vote.

Band, Simon (Forward): Born 1/1/1977 in Macclesfield.

A strong centre forward known for his work rate, he had a big engine and never stopped running. During his career he played for Bollington Athletic, Congleton Town, and a brief spell at

Trafford before moving to Atherton LR for the 2003/4 season.

Whilst at Atherton LR his strength shone through and he scored a brace in the Hospital Cup game, including an extra time winner to put Atherton LR into the semi-finals.

He played in the friendly game against Woodley Sports, scoring in the 4-2 win, and also in the benefit game for Jamie Turner v AFC Telford in May 2006.

He made an impressive debut for FC United against Daisy Hill in the 3-0 victory.

BBC: The BBC programme 'Inside Out' was nominated for two awards for its film about FC United. The awards for national and regional Royal Television Society Awards mean that the film was one of the best three sports films made in Britain last year.

Benefit Matches: FC United as a community-based club take part in many benefit matches. Jamie Turner was the first, but FC United played in a benefit match against Stalybridge Celtic and against an all stars team for Chris McGuirk.

 FC United together with AFC Telford arranged a benefit match for a life-long Manchester United supporter, Jamie Turner. Jamie was the victim of a vicious unprovoked armed attack on his way to St Mary's in Southampton which left him suffering a fractured skull, a pooling of blood in the brain which required immediate brain surgery and in a coma clinging to life. His two-month stay in hospital, three weeks of which he remained in a coma, included craniotomy and tracheotomy operations and surgery.

Jamie has been left with poor vision in his left eye, extremely painful headaches and fatigued at the slightest exertions. Jamie has survived the initial ordeal but the road to recovery will be long and painful. As he is self-employed, his family relied greatly on his income. FC United's portion of the gate receipts were donated to the Jamie Turner Fund, helping to raise more than £6,000. The match was played on Saturday 6th May 2005, with AFC Telford running out 3-0 winners in front of the Turner family and 1,359 fans.

Bhopal Medical Appeal: FC United's main sponsor set up a sports club for the benefit of the children of the gas-affected town and two sets of kits were sent to them from the Kit Aid Day.

Blatter, Sepp: FIFA President and a huge fan of lower league football gave FC United an interview. Questions were sent to him via e-mail and he found time in his busy schedule to reply.

BMW: Replaced Bhopal as the club's main sponsor for the 2006/7 season.

Board Members: At the EGM in July 2005 the following were elected onto the board:

Adam Brown: works in the sports research department at Manchester Metropolitan University. A former committee member of the Independent Manchester United Supporters Association (IMUSA) and a former Old Trafford season ticket holder, he has also been a member of the Football Supporters Association's national committee.

Russell Delaney: an independent financial adviser who had specialised in the football industry. A Manchester United supporter for 40 years he had contacts at all levels of the game.

Scott Fletcher: a child actor who starred in football drama 'Jossy's Giants' and now runs a multi-million pound IT solutions company which he started from scratch 10 years ago. He cancelled his four corporate seats at Old Trafford in protest at Glazer's takeover.

Martin Morris: a contributor to 'United We Stand' fanzine and was involved in FCUoM from the start, helping with kit selection, pledges and liaison with other clubs.

Pete Munday: works in finance and was a mover behind developing the business plan which FC United had to present to the North West Counties League committee before being accepted – was also a member of IMUSA and Shareholders United.

Tony Pritchard: acting chairman of FCUoM who owns his own food manufacturing firm. Pritchard was heavily involved in devising the business plan and in ground-share negotiations.

Phil Sheeran: as a manager at the Apollo Theatre in Manchester, has worked for years in ticketing, crowd and operations management. He helped to bring about the public rally at the Apollo which led to the formation of FC United in the summer.

Jules Spencer: former chair of IMUSA and now FC United's press officer, he works in local government in Rochdale.

Joseph Tully: a corporate and commercial lawyer who has worked in the leisure industry for the last eight years and is now using his legal skills to FC's advantage.

Vasco Wackrill: resigned from Manchester United's fans' forum in the wake of the Glazer family's takeover, and has been responsible for co-ordinating the 4,000 financial pledges FC received, setting up online donations and membership database.

Andy Walsh: is another former chair of IMUSA. Walsh was a leading light in the fight against both Rupert Murdoch and Glazer, and is now acting general manager of FCUM.

The Chairman has yet to be chosen; meanwhile, Tony Pritchard is acting Chair. The Board also resolved that the club required the services of two full-time employees as the club could not function properly with only part-time support. Two temporary roles were created to allow time for the positions to be advertised properly and for employment practice to be followed. The role of Acting Chairman was also created in order for the Board to consider who should be appointed to the position on a permanent basis. There are only 2 employees at the club: Andy Walsh, who is Acting General Manager of the club, and Luc Zentar was appointed as Acting Club Secretary with Tony Pritchard appointed as Acting Club Chairman.

The roles of General Manager and Club Secretary are full-time paid positions, and Acting Chairman is not.

At the October board meeting, the details of the positions were finalised for the permanent full-time posts. Board members are selected for a two-year period, with half of the board being re-elected yearly. Just who steps down is drawn by lots.

Football Club United of Manchester
Created from despair - Powered by passion

Brandao, Ricardo (Forward):

Reserve Squad.

Ricardo was in the historic side that played in the first ever game for the reserves. The friendly played against Flint Town United was won 1-0, with Ricardo passing on the final ball to strike partner Gary Edwards to score the only goal of the game with a crisply taken shot in front of 900 travelling fans.

In September 2006, Ricardo was invited to join the England squad to play in the Homeless World Cup to be held in South Africa.

He was released by the club in December 2006 to join Oldham Town.

Brennan, Stuart: Stuart is a reporter for the *Manchester Evening News* and was presented with the 'Football Writers Award' for his quality reporting and coverage of the sports affairs in Manchester, in particular his writing on the birth of FC United of Manchester. He was presented with the award at Gigg Lane prior to an FC United game in July 2006.

Brown, David (Defender): Born 15/9/1972 in Bolton.

Dave's pedigree had been seen by Arsenal as a 9-year-old, but the law stated that you had to be 14 years old before you could sign forms and Manchester United scouts had made their interests known in him as a 13-year-old, so there was only one club Dave was going to join.

Dave was a trainee striker at Manchester United FC who was the last junior signed by big Ron Atkinson. He signed professional forms for the club in 1986. David spent three years at Old Trafford until May 1988, when Sir Alex Ferguson decided not to keep any of the juniors and made a loan period to Hull City permanent.

He had been offered a trial at Rochdale, but Dave declined; instead opting for college and more qualifications.

He had spells at Torquay, briefly before spending six months at Chester City, a season at Telford United, Hereford United, Accrington Stanley and Burton United and even a spell in Canada! A number of appearances for non-league clubs followed: Leigh RMI, Mossley, a team that he had three spells with and whose appearances and skill saw him earn the captain's armband, Bacup Borough, Castleton Gabriels, then Salford City. It was at Salford City he met up with future team-mates Karl, Tony Cullen, Billy McCartney and Phil Melville.

He was also voted Player of the Year and made captain. He moved onto Radcliffe Borough after politics saw the manager released and some of the team followed out of loyalty. After Radcliffe Borough he joined Mossley for the last of his three spells before he settled at FC United. A regular playing partner of captain Dave Chadwick, together they make a formidable defensive duo. A 'no nonsense' player with top-flight experience who began as a striker and as the legs tired became a defender.

He scored on his first start for FC United in a hard fought 2-1 away win against Darwen. Dave left the club early in September 2006 to join Salford City to play regular first team football, but re-joined FC United in October 2006 and scored again on his 'debut'.

He finally hung up his boots at the end of the 2006/7 season, when FC United were promoted to the UniBond Northern Premier League, playing his last game against Formby.

Bury: Bury Football Club was founded on 24th April 1885 after a public meeting held at the White Horse Hotel. A committee was formed and the club became sub-tenants of a field on Gigg Lane, which belonged to the Earl of Derby. It became the club's home.

Four months later a team was assembled and on 5th September 1885 Bury played their first game: a friendly, resulting in a draw 2-2 away against Little Lever. The following week, Bury beat Wigan 4-3 in their first home fixture. Bury competed only in friendlies until 1889, when the club was instrumental in creating the Lancashire League.

The Shakers – a nickname given to the team by Chairman J T Ingham, having announced at the start of a Lancashire Senior Cup game, "We'll give 'em a shaking. In fact, we are the Shakers!"

In May 1894 Bury applied for membership of the Football League and joined Division Two and in the September they played their first ever league game. The Shakers then won all fifteen home games, winning the Division Two Championship at the first attempt. Being Champions didn't automatically mean promotion to Division One. Bury had to beat Liverpool, who were bottom of Division One.

Bury stayed in Division One for eleven years, but were finally relegated at the end of 1911/12 season.

Bury gained perhaps its greatest achievement when they won the FA Cup twice within three years.

In 1900 they beat Southampton 4-0 and in 1903 they beat Derby County by a record 6-0.

Between 1912 and 1924 the Shakers stayed In Division Two, but enjoyed a spell in Division One for five seasons between 1924 and 1929. In the 1925/6 season, Bury finished fourth. Bury were relegated to Division Two in 1929 and remained there until 1957. For the first time in the club's history, Bury were demoted to the lower leagues, playing a season in Division Three North during 1957/58 season.

In 1960/61 season Bury clinched the Division Three championship and the 1960s brought a further seven seasons in the old Second Division, which ended in 1969; but by 1971 the club had been relegated to Division Four and was facing financial difficulties. Promotion from Division Four followed in 1973/74 and the Shakers remained in Division Three throughout the 1970s.

Bury were relegated again in 1980, but bounced back in the 1984/85 season, clinching promotion in the club's centenary year, despite having a very small team. Only 16 players were used and the reserve team was scrapped to save money. Bury faced relegation again at the end of 1991/92 season and lack of finances meant the sale of several first team players. Gradually the club's fortunes were turned around and the wooden Gigg Lane stadium was re-built on three sides.

On the field Bury made it to the Division Three play-off final in 1995, but the Shakers lost 2-0. The following year, after a dismal start, the club climbed from 23rd in Division Three to claim promotion in the final home game of the season.

Football Club United of Manchester
Created from despair - Powered by passion

In the 1996/97 season, Bury defied the odds to claim the Division Two title – only the third in the club's history and back-to-back promotions.

A combination of money problems and the enforced sale of players meant that Bury suffered relegation from Division One in May 1999 –but only on 'goals scored'. Bury needed one more goal to survive the drop. Financial difficulties in the 2000/01 season saw the club put up for sale by the High Court, with no

money available and only the free transfer of a Liverpool striker saved the Shakers from certain relegation as they ended a sixteen-game run of defeats.

The new Cemetery End stand marked the completion of the re-development of Gigg Lane into today's 11,500 all-seated stadium. The 2001/02 season was traumatic for Gigg Lane. In March 2002 the club was placed in administration after a takeover bid failed. With crippling debts and decreased gates, the only option open to Bury was administration. The club was saved from extinction by the efforts of the supporters, but were relegated to Division Three. But the fact that the club started the new season is a testament to the efforts behind it.

Gordon Sorfleet, the club's press officer, was awarded the UEFA Supporter of the year award for 2002 at a glittering gala in Monaco.

Bury finished the 2002/03 season with a play-off semi-final at Bournemouth, but a bad performance saw Bury crash out to face another season in the third division and players were released. Before the 2002/03 season began, the Shakers announced a new chairman. But the 2004/05 season saw the Shakers finish in their lowest ever league position and again financial problems arose. The 2005/06 season began with the newly-formed club FC United of Manchester ground sharing.

Bushel, Lee:

Reserve Squad.

Lee was named in the squad to face Kirkham and Wesham in the July 2006 friendly fixture.

Byrne, Luke (Forward):

He had a brief spell at FC United, being listed as a substitute for the friendly game against Flixton in August 2005, but didn't stay and joined Trafford instead. He was in the squad to play against AFC Wimbledon for the Supporters Direct Cup in July 2005.

C

Cancelled Games: St Helens Town cancelled a friendly game against FC United after a steward was allegedly assaulted during the good-natured pitch invasion following the 0-0 draw against Leigh RMI.

(No league games have been cancelled.)

Cantona, Eric: The Old Trafford legend gave his backing to FC United, saying he would never work at OT whilst the Americans owned the club and agreed with the fans who refused to bankroll the takeover through the turnstiles, instead creating another club to channel their football passion. He said, "I agree with the fans. Because who's interest do the fans have in doing that? It's for the passion and the love of the game and their love for the club. So I have the same feeling as them."

Captains: FCUoM have had seven captains in its short history. Billy McCartney had the honour of being FCUoM's first team captain in a friendly against Leigh RMI. The Captain's armband was worn by Tony Coyne for the Stalybridge Celtic friendly and Mark Rawlinson for the Supporters Direct Cup game against AFC Wimbledon. The role has since been taken over by Dave Chadwick, though the Captain's armband was worn by Dave Brown and Rory Patterson during Chadwick's absence.

In the 2nd qualifying round match against Brodsworth MW, Liam Coyne deputised in the absence of Dave Chadwick.

Carden, Simon (Midfielder): Born 26/10/1978 in Stretford, Manchester.

Simon started playing football at an early age and played for the Stretford Vics U7s and continued playing for them until he was 16 years old. In that time he saw players such as Danny Higginbotham and Jamie Wood, both ex-Manchester United players, come and go.

Simon had a chance to join MUFC as Brian Kidd used to do the training sessions, but instead in 1994 he went for trials at Liverpool and Nottingham Forest. He sufficiently impressed

Stockport County with his goal-scoring ability that they offered him a 2-year Youth Training Scheme. He progressed and was signed on professional forms for a year. Unfortunately, a change of management meant that his contract wasn't renewed at the end of the 1997/98 season. Picking himself up, he went for trials with Portsmouth but ended up settling down with Radcliffe Borough. He signed for Radcliffe Borough, scoring 22 goals in the 1999/00 season, before transferring to Accrington Stanley in December 2000 for £5,000 and scoring on his debut! He then re-joined Radcliffe Borough on loan in July 2003 after an injury kept him out of the side, helping gain promotion into the Conference. Simon was offered an extension to stay at Accrington Stanley but he declined, preferring to play football regularly, and he re-joined Radcliffe Borough. Alas, a disagreement meant that his stay was short-lived, leaving in December 2004. He left football and had surgery on his knee. After speaking to his former team mate and close friend Joz Mitten about FC United, a club he thought was a wind-up, he spoke to the manager Karl – another former team mate – and even though he wasn't fully fit he agreed to sign up. He signed for FCUoM on 18th August 2005, where his goal-scoring talents became more apparent, netting 5 times in one game in a 10-2 victory.

As well as having goal-scoring records, he also has the unfortunate record of being the first player to be yellow carded in a home game. He scored 18 goals in all competitions in the team's first season.

In FC United's first FA Vase away game to old foe Padiham in October 2006 Simon continued his scoring talents by bagging a brace in the 3-0 win.

Football Club United of Manchester
Created from despair - Powered by passion

Simon Carden

Celebrity Match: Macclesfield Town hold fond memories for a number of FC United players. Manager Karl Marginson and his assistant manager Phil Power as well as Darren Lyons played for the club and when Macclesfield Town required help and a Celebrity All Stars versus Macclesfield Legends was arranged, Phil Power and Darren Lyons turned out to help and played along side Sammy McIlroy against an all-star side that included Gianfranco Zola, Gus Poyet, and Manchester United favourites Bryan Robson, Mark Hughes and Viv Anderson. Phil rolled back the years, played the full 90 minutes, scored a hat trick in front of 5,000-plus fans, and deservedly picked up the 'Man of the Match' award in the 5-2 victory. Around £50,000 was raised for Macclesfield Town that evening.

Century: Josh Howard scored FC United's 100th goal in competitive football when he scored FC United's first goal away at Norton United. FC United won 3-1, gaining revenge as Norton were the first team to inflict defeat on FC United. The goal didn't come until the 25th minute in the reverse fixture on 9th April 2006.

Rhodri Giggs has the honour of scoring FC United's one hundredth goal in Division One, courtesy of a fine touch in the 6-2 victory over Colne on 3rd March 2007.

Chadwick, David (Defender): Born 17/9/1977 in Wigan.

Referred to as being 'my Stevie Bruce' by manager Karl Marginson and a lovely guy to boot, Dave had played alongside Karl at Salford City. 'Chaddy' played for Southport FC in 1994, played for Atherton LR in February 1999 and won a cap for Lancashire U18s.

Having played alongside Dave, Karl had no hesitation in inviting him to play for FC United.   A solid, no-nonsense defender who could also score his fair share of goals made Dave a must for the team.

Dave chose to watch his new colleagues in action before donning the shirt or wearing the captain's armband and it was arranged for him to go to the Wimbledon game on one of the coaches.

Turning out in front of 2,500 hysterical fans each week is every footballer's dream and 'Chaddy' is no different, so he had no qualms about joining. Signed for FCUoM after the beginning of the season from Prescott Cables and was immediately made captain.

He was Prescott Cables' 'Player of the Year' for the previous 2 years running, as well as being the manager's 'Player of the Year', the players' 'Player of the Year' and the supporters' 'Player of the Year'.

Dave made his debut in the home fixture against Padiham FC.

His dedication and commitment to the club and the fans made him a popular member of FC United.

Has the dubious honour of being the first FC player to be booked in the FA Vase competition.

Dave Chadwick

Football Club United of Manchester
Created from despair - Powered by passion

Champions: North West Counties Football League (NWCFL).

Division One Champions 2006/7.

Division Two Champions 2005/6.

Charity: A group of FC United supporters ran in the Great Manchester 10km Run to celebrate FC United's first season, but also to raise money for a local charity. The runners ran in the full FC United of Manchester strip.

Cheadle Town: FC United's first official cup game was against Cheadle Town of the same league on 17th October. Cheadle Town were formed in 1961 as Grasmere Rovers, playing Sundays in a Manchester Junior League. The club then joined the Manchester League in 1972, which allowed them to play on Saturdays. Glory followed with manager Albert Pike when they won both the Manchester and Derbyshire FA Cups. It was in 1982 that Grasmere Rovers moved to their own ground at Park Road Stadium and a year later changed their name to Cheadle Town. This coincided with them joining the North West Counties League Division Three for the 1983/84 season. The 1987/88 season saw Division Three absorbed into Division Two. Cheadle Town were promoted in 1997/98 but were relegated after two seasons. FC United won the game 5-1.

Clean Sheets: In their inaugural season, goalie Barrie George kept 10 clean sheets, 9 in the league and 1 cup game. Phil Melville kept 3 in the league.

Sam Ashton kept 21 clean sheets for the 2006/7 season: 17 in the league and 4 in the two cup competitions. John Ogden kept 1 clean sheet in a league game.

Coaching: As part of the policy of making live football accessible to every fan, and in order to give back something to the community, FC United have launched a coaching school. Beginning in the November, for a couple of hours on Sunday afternoons over a 7-week period, FA-approved coaches as well as FC United players were on hand to give a helping hand to aspiring footballers.

Collier, Warren (Defender): Born 13/6/1986 in Stretford, Manchester.

Reserve Squad.

Warren began his football career with the famous Stretford Victoria club and scoring goals for the under 12s. He then played for Monton Amateurs in the East Manchester League for three years, scoring regularly. First team manager Karl Marginson was so impressed by Collier that he sought permission from Monton to give him a trial at FC United. He signed for FC United but will continue to play for Monton Amateurs, making some impressive performances.

He is a versatile player who has played in midfield and has been described as a 'tricky winger'. He impressed during the friendly against Glossop North End on Wednesday 8th February 2006 and scored a cracker. He was also named in the squad to face Kirkham and Wesham in a friendly match in July 2006. He was signed in time for the game against Daisy Hill on 11th February, though he didn't make his debut until 19th April 2006 away to Chadderton.   Warren topped the reserves goal-scoring chart.

Colne: The first team to beat FCUoM in a cup game, winning 2-1 on 13th November 2005 in the 2nd Round of the League Challenge Cup. Colne took the lead against the run of play and appeared to be through to the next round until Steve Torpey equalised in the 90th minute. Colne regained the lead from the kick-off and held on to win. FCUoM did well against a team placed a division higher than themselves and were unlucky not to win, having had a goal disallowed in the first half.

Community: As part of FCUoM's policy of being a community football club, they made a guest appearance at the Thorn Cross Youth Offenders Institution. A match played behind closed doors for obvious reasons was won 7-1 by FCUoM. Thorn Cross is a purpose-built open youth offender institute with 316 rooms. The youths here have less than 2 years to serve and the programme includes the provision of farms and gardens and other training courses. Parent craft, drug awareness, anger management, car crime and help to stop smoking courses are available through a YMCA-led course. Also available are Offending Behaviour Programmes. A resettlement programme for job/training placement and mentoring are on offer to the housemates. The establishment meant more to some players than others and some stayed behind to talk to the youngsters after the game.

Competitive Football: The first FC United footballer to kick a ball in competitive football was Barrie George, as he collected a through ball from Leek CSOB's back line moments after Leek had kicked-off the first game in FC United's history.

Contract: There are only a few players signed on a contract: Jonathan Mitten, Steve Torpey and Dave Chadwick. Karl Marginson was able to add Josh Howard and Simon Carden on contracts in January 2006. Simon signed until the end of the 2005/06 season and Joshua until the end of 2006/07 season. Should a club come in for a contracted player then the clubs can negotiate a fee.

Cooney, Mark: Physiotherapist.

Complaint: FCUoM considered making their first formal complaint in November 2005. The complaint laid against Darwen FC was for greed. Darwen priced the tickets at £6 for all tickets and no concessions, which meant that FCUoM's younger fans would have to pay three times more than normal. This goes against the FCUoM policy and, despite requests from the FCUoM board, Darwen refused to back down, claiming that they wouldn't be able to verify who would be eligible for concessions. FCUoM understood that their many travelling fans gave many clubs a welcome cash injection but also a headache because of the need for increased safety and security. Most clubs have responded by discussing the safety arrangements and concessions, and put into place the appropriate procedure. A problem solved by using common sense. Following the game, the players and management indicated their displeasure by declining the food and drink offered to them as is standard practice for visiting teams and departed directly after the match.

Coronation Street: The hugely popular and apparently timeless soap has a link to FC United: Ken Barlow's television son Adam, actor Sam Robertson, has appeared for the reserves and starred in the 2-1 win over Abbey Hey. He appeared in 113 episodes between 2004 and 2007.

Cosgrave, Martin (Midfielder).

Reserve Squad.

Martin has the honour of scoring the winning goal in the league game that saw them beat Padiham 1-0 and clinch the league title at the first time of asking.

Coyne, Liam (Defender): Born 8/5/1987 in Stretford.

Football became a richer world when Liam decided to play football instead of Gaelic football. He had played Gaelic football, following in the footsteps of his grandfather, father and older brothers, and even played alongside Will Ahern before changing allegiances. So, as a 6-year-old he played football at St Brendan's and joined the under 10s, but after a while he joined St Ann's, a team set up by his father and a friend.

Liam gained so much experience playing at levels above his age group that he won just about every honour going, playing for the

Lancashire County Youth side, where he captained the successful side.

Eventually, he sought a new challenge and joined Urmston Town as a 13-year-old and thoroughly enjoyed the buzz of scoring goals; and his height gave him a huge advantage. It was when he wanted to join a Monday night training session that he changed position to defence. The coach, Andy Nelson, didn't believe that this giant of a striker was only 13, so Liam collected his father and birth certificate and went back. Nelson was convinced and put Liam in defence, using his height and strength to terrify attackers. Liam became so comfortable in defence that he earned the plaudits of Nelson and he was invited for a trial at Rochdale. Going through the elimination process was hard work, but Coyne passed and was in the squad playing against such teams as Bradford and Wigan for the under 15s. Alas, he was released after a few months and the affair put him off football for a while. Coach Nelson persuaded Liam to forget the incident and learn from it and, as a result, Liam joined Trafford FC.

Meanwhile, Andy Nelson became reserve team manager at Leigh RMI and one of the first players Nelson contacted to join him was Liam. 16-year-old Liam joined and forced his way into the first team, making his debut in front of 4,000 fans against Halifax Town and earned the 'man of the match' award.

It was a few months before he was selected again and, being eager to please, he managed to get sent off. Despite this setback and the spiralling fortunes of Leigh RMI, who went through 4 managers and two relegations in quick succession, Leigh RMI offered him a 1-year contract after hearing that Premiership side Chelsea were watching him.

Liam was delighted to sign, but the contract prevented him from

Football Club United of Manchester
Created from despair - Powered by passion

joining FC United, a team he had heard about from Will Ahern – but, being the professional he was, he fought 100% for Leigh RMI and when he wasn't offered an extension he left; and after a call from Karl Marginson he teamed up with FC United for pre-season training.

His enormous talent and willingness to fight won the manager over and Liam joined FC United, waiting in the wings to fight for his place with stalwarts such as Dave Chadwick and Rob Nugent. He was on the bench for the Supporters Direct Cup in July and made his debut in the opening league game against St Helen's Town and scored his first goal for the club against Bacup Borough in September 2006, coming on as a substitute. Unfortunately, he was sent of in the FA Carlsberg Cup game against Quorn FC and found it hard to gain his place back. He captained the side in the 2nd qualifying round game against Brodsworth MW.

In February 2007 he re-joined Leigh RMI to help them fight for league status. He had brief spells at Winsford United where he won player of the month for May and a spell at Warrington Town, though he remains registered as a FC United player.

Coyne, Tony (Midfielder): Born 12/3/1978 in Manchester.
Tony joined FC United from Trafford. A hard-working midfielder known for his graft and intelligent use of the ball, during one spell at Mossley he played in every single position on the park!
He spent most of his football career at Mossley, but he plied his trade with Cheadle Town in the late 90s before a brief stint at Flixton and in the early 2000s Woodley Sports, before returning to Cheadle Town via a spell at Mossley.
Tony's talents were rewarded by being included in the Greater Manchester U19s side in the Premier League Quarter-Final.

He spent a season here before again appearing for Flixton, along with Sammy McIlroy, an ex-Manchester United icon, and then a short stay at Trafford.

For the 2002/3 season he re-signed for Mossley, where he won three 'Man of the Match' awards, scored 5 goals (including a hat-trick) and was presented with the 'Supporters Club Player of the Month' award in August 2003.

He finally left Mossley in February 2005 after making 143 appearances and scoring 21 goals and joined Trafford again. He didn't stop long, as he'd heard about FC United being formed and he wanted to play his part. He joined FC United and took part in FC United's first ever game of football against Leigh RMI and then played in the Supporters Direct Cup.

He made his debut for FC United against Leek CSOB after having played in the pre season friendlies. Tony's father is Peter Coyne, who played for Manchester United and Crewe Alexandria.

Tony left the club in March 2006 and joined Flixton.

Croft, Alex: A lovely lad who the fans at FC United took to their hearts.

Alex suffers with a number of illnesses which require constant attention and he is wheelchair-bound. The fans took to the streets in Manchester and ran 10km in order to raise money for the lad and the equipment he needed. Alex is probably FC United's number 1 fan!

Cups:

League Championship Cup: FC United's first promotion silverware. Promoted on 12th April 2006, and celebrated being champions on 15th, when their nearest rivals lost. A proud captain, Dave Chadwick, lifted the trophy after the Great Harwood game on Saturday 22nd April 2006.

The Supporters Direct Trust Cup: Supporters Direct was established in late 2000 following a report to the Government's Football Taskforce.   It allows supporters to join together and buy into and influence the running of their own clubs.   AFC Wimbledon, another club created by the fans, hosted this year's game and only just beat FC United, winning 0-1. This cup has previously been challenged for by Brentford and Enfield Town, clubs who are owned or operated by their fans. There is a possibility of it becoming an annual fixture.

FC United gained revenge for the defeat by winning 2-1 in the following year.

League Challenge Cup: 1st round, 15th October 2005 (later postponed and re-arranged for 17th October at a new venue). FCUoM played Cheadle Town in the first round, winning 5-1, before losing 2-1 away to Colne in round two.

The following season FC United won the League Challenge Cup on 3rd May 2007, beating Curzon Ashton 2-1 and completing a league and cup double.

League Challenge Cup Squad

Division Two Cup: Open to all 19 teams, consisting of 4 rounds: 1st and 2nd round, a two-legged semi-final and final. FCUoM were given a bye into round 2, where they faced New Mills on 3rd December away from home. FC United won 5-0, with Steve Torpey scoring a hat-trick. They were beaten 1-0 by Nelson FC after extra time in the quarter-finals.

Reserves Division Cup: The reserve side won the Cup, beating old rivals Padiham 4-1.

Cullen, Tony (Defender): Born 25/9/1973 in Salford.

Tony was a keen footballer from an early age, not only playing for his primary and then secondary schools but for Bar Hill on Sundays. Bar Hill was one of the top sides in Manchester and

Football Club United of Manchester
Created from despair - Powered by passion

scouts from the local clubs were often on the look-out for new talent. Tony stayed at Bar Hill until his middle teens, when his talent, determination and discipline learnt at Bar Hill got him noticed by scouts from the Salford Boys Team and it was whilst at Salford Boys that Tony was one of a number of lads selected to play at Manchester United's School of Excellence. His stay at Manchester lasted a few years and he trained with the likes of Ryan Giggs. Competition at Manchester was stiff and with new players coming along Tony felt that his chance of playing first team football lay elsewhere. He had already drawn attention from other clubs and he was offered a Youth Training Scheme (YTS) place at Blackburn Rovers and he moved on. Unfortunately, after the two years he wasn't offered a contract and Aston Villa, who had been keeping tabs on the midfielder, offered him training facilities and a tour of Switzerland with the under 21s, playing alongside Dwight Yorke, and he performed well. He was invited back pre-season but Ron Atkinson was only prepared to offer Tony a month-by-month contract, which meant very little football. Disheartened, he left Villa and football.

A tinkering with non-league Mossley followed in 1992/3, but it was five years before an old mate, Loz Greenhalgh, persuaded him to put on his boots again and he signed for Radcliffe Borough and for the next couple of seasons he played settled football. The manager was so popular that he was offered a job by Salford City and he left the club, taking with him a number of specially selected players; Tony Cullen was one of them. The next few seasons at Salford were good and the team were on the brink of greatness when a managerial breakdown meant that the manager left and a few of the players followed. The team had narrowly failed to gain promotion and were in the final of the prestigious Manchester County Premier Cup for the first time in their history.

The briefest of time was spent at Altrincham. He signed for them in March 2003 but due to injury didn't make his debut until a few weeks later, when he came on for the last three minutes of extra time in a cup game. He left in the April.

Another brief stint followed, this time at Monton Amateurs for the 2003/4 season.

Tony called time on his football career only to make a come-back on the strength of his trip to watch a friendly game between FC United and Flixton.

The manager, Karl Marginson, had found the midfield maestro and invited him to the friendly and when he saw the set-up and the quality of the football he was eager to play again. Karl joked that had he known then he would've given him a game, only to be told his boots were in the car! Tony played in the second half and joined FC United.

Tony made his debut in the 4-0 away win over Ashton Town.

On 5th April 2006, FC United were proud to announce that Tony – who was taking his coaching badges – had been offered and had accepted the position of Reserve Team Manager for the season 2006/07 and he retired from first team football.

The reserve team won their division at the first try with three games to spare and also made it through to the Reserve Cup Final on 9th May 2007, winning 1-0 and completing a league and cup double.

Football Club United of Manchester
Created from despair - Powered by passion

Curzon Ashton: Their Tameside Stadium was used by Cheadle Town to play FC United as a venue for the re-arranged League Challenge Cup game.

Curzon Ashton's ground was selected to host the NWCFL Cup Final on 3rd May 2007 and, as luck would have it, Curzon were also FC United's first Cup Final opponents.

Curry Club: The Curry Club is a wonderful way to prepare for a match. FCUoM chef Tracy Maun provides a delicious curry before home games to season ticket holders and up to two guests, all for a fiver. Between 30 and 70 supporters enjoy her culinary delights.

D

Departures: The first player to leave FCUoM was Phil Priestley, the goalkeeper. Barrie George had taken over the number 1 jersey and Phil was unable to claim it back. Phil left in September 2005.

Defeats:

League: The first league home defeat was against Norton United and came on the back of six league wins and a draw. FC United lost three league games in their inaugural season all at home, including the last home game.

FC United didn't lose an away league game all season.

Highest: The biggest league defeat was at the hands of Atherton Collieries on 29th November 2006, when they lost 0-3 at home in the 2006/07 season.

Cup Defeat: Colne were the first team to beat FC United in the 2nd round of the League Challenge Cup. Colne were in Division One of the North West Counties Football League at the time, some 13 places above FC United.

Division Two Cup: The first team to beat FC United in the Division Two Cup were Nelson on 4th February 2006, gaining revenge for the two league defeats inflicted by FC United.

Delayed Kick-Offs: A number of games home and away had their kick-offs delayed, mainly for safety reasons. However, the away game to Oldham Town almost wasn't played at all. An hour before kick-off, Oldham's secretary, Dave Shepherd, noticed the lack of match officials. Mr Shepherd rang the appointed referee, Mark Bailey, who was at home and explained that he had been informed by the referees' association that the game was off. Embarrassed League officials praised Mr Shepherd's quick thinking in getting four match officials ready at such short notice and promised an investigation into the blunder. Referee Derek Brannick had gone to the game as a spectator and had to rush home to get his gear and three others came from Castleton, Stretford and Ramsbottom.

Development Fund: One of the features surrounding FC United

Football Club United of Manchester

Created from despair - Powered by passion

and its structure is to have their own ground, a place to call their own, a home. Many fund-raising initiatives have taken place, such as 5-a-side tournaments, bingo evenings, auctions and the like. A group of fans attended the Pack Horse PH for an evening of entertaining football 'a la Playstation' in the form of a Pro-Evo Tournament. The evening raised £100 towards the fund and the winner was presented with a trophy before the Formby game by one of the players.

Double, League and Cup: FC United completed a league and cup double in the 2006/7 season in the NWCFL Division One, the first in their history and the third in the history of the NWCFL.

Doubles: FC United's first league double came from victories over Castleton Gabriels, 10-2 at home and 0-3 away. FC United also recorded home and away victories over Darwen, Nelson, Ashton Town, Daisy Hill, Blackpool Mechanics, Holker Old Boys, Leek CSOB, Oldham Town, New Mills, Chadderton FC and Padiham FC. In total, FC United achieved the double over 12 clubs in the 2005/6 season.

In the 2006/7 season they went even better and did the 'double' over 15 clubs.

Draws:

First: The first official game in FC United's history began with a draw away to Leigh RMI, a team placed some divisions higher than themselves. The friendly took place in front of 2,500 fans on

81

16th July 2005.

The inaugural season saw 6 draws in total: 5 league and 1 cup.

FC United were held to 4 draws in the 2006/7 season and they were all score draws.

Away: The first league draw was away to Winsford United 2-2 on 31st August 2005.

The first away draw in Division One was against Congleton Town in December 2006 when they were held to a 1-1 draw.

Home: FC United's first league home draw was against Cheadle Town on 1st April 2006 when FC United came back from a goal down to share the points.

It wasn't until the end of April 2007 that FC United suffered a home draw: 4-4 against Trafford in the 2006/7 season.

Cup, Away: The first scoreless cup game was in the League Challenge Cup away at Eccleshall on 5th November 2005.

FC United drew 2-2 away to old foe Congleton Town in the first leg semi-final of the League Challenge Cup in March 2007 in the 2006/7 season.

Cup, Home: No draws in any home cup games in the first or second seasons.

Droylsden FC: When FCUoM were accepted into the North West Counties League Second Division of the competition, Dave Pace, a long-time Manchester United fan and chairman/manager of Droylsden, offered Droylsden FC's Butcher's Arms Ground to ground share. This was subject to council approval. The Conference North side have a stadium with a capacity of 3,500. Permission was, however, not granted and FCUoM began the search for another venue.

DVD: DVDs were recorded of the first league away game against Leek CSOB. Since then, FC United have released an official mid-season DVD of the first half of the season containing 93 minutes of action from 14 games, 51 goals, fans clips and a short bonus film of 'The People versus Malcolm Glazer'.

E

Easter, Matt:
Reserve Squad.
Matt was named in the reserve squad that lost to Kirkham and Wesham in July 2006.

Edwards, Gary (Forward):
Reserve Squad.

Gary was in the historic side that played in the first ever game for the reserves. The friendly played against Flint Town United was won 1-0, with striker Gary scoring the only goal of the game with a crisply taken shot in front of 900 travelling fans, and so he went into the record books for scoring the first goal in the reserve team's history. Edwards joined the club from Bury Amateurs after taking part in the summer trials and becoming a prolific striker. He played in the opening game of the season, scoring in the 7-0 win over Padiham in August 2006.

Ellis, Lee (Forward):

Reserve Squad.

Lee played for Moston Junior U15s in the Manchester County FA Youth Cup, scoring a brace, and knows the joys of victory. His team mate and also goal scorer is Dominic Stockdale.

Elvin, Kevin (Defender): Born 22/5/1979 in Coventry.

Kevin joined Coventry's top junior side in an attempt to realise his dream to become a footballer. He was just 8-years-old when he joined Chapelfield Colts.

He soon switched to Birmingham City Juniors, whose facilities were better, before he tried to earn himself a Youth Training Scheme (YTS) contract.

However, he didn't pursue the contract, instead favouring to gain an education and studying. He maintained his love of football by joining Nuneaton Borough just after they had won the Southern League Midland Division title and the Southern League Cup in the 1995/6 season.

After one season and despite being told he was part of the future plans for the club, he could see that the club's success would attract more players and that competition for places would be even more difficult, so he decided to leave.

Kevin continued his university education but still maintained his contact with football and played for local sides like Sutton Coldfield Town and Atherstone United and even after his graduation in 2000 he never stayed longer than a season, serving such clubs as Stratford Town and Racing Club Warwick

Football Club United of Manchester
Created from despair - Powered by passion

before moving on.

Even though his football was part-time, he went on a tour of Australia, where he impressed the local Sydney scout so much he was invited to stay and play for the winter with Australia's top club, AC United. He enjoyed the warm winter but after a season he was on his way back to England and settled down with his girlfriend in Manchester, where he continued to play 5-a-side football, where again his talent was spotted by a local scout who passed on his details to Karl Marginson.

Kevin was invited to trial with FC United and after the eliminating process had finished he found himself in the squad. He impressed sufficiently to be named for the game against Leigh RMI and, despite getting lost, arriving late, and being dropped in favour of Billy McCartney, he still managed to get a game after replacing Billy McCartney, who received an injury, and kept his place in the side for the start of the season.

He was credited with scoring FCUoM's first own goal in a friendly against Flixton FC, but after starting 8 out of the 10 league and cup games the side were undefeated.

He left FC United in November 2006 to join Monton Amateurs to regain fitness after a knee injury, but eventually left the club to join Trafford in March 2007, having made 22 appearances in the inaugural season, his last being the cup game against Nelson.

EUFA Cup: Whilst FCUoM have not made any appearances in the EUFA Cup, Phil Priestley has. He appeared as goalkeeper for

Bangor City in 1994.

Europe: FC United played their first friendly in East Germany after their first season was over. Their hosts, Lokomotive Leipzig FC, are also a fan-run club after the original club folded because of corruption and the fans created the new club. The fixture took place at Bruno Plache Stadium on 12th May 2006.

Around 1,000 FC United fans made up the 7,462 attendance figure, with Dave Swarbrick scoring FC United's first overseas goal in an entertaining 4-4 draw.

The other scorers that night were Rob Nugent, Rory Patterson (pen) and Simon Carden. Rob Nugent also scored an own goal!

Ever-Presents: Rob Nugent has played in 32 league and 4 cup games, making 3 more league appearances than Steve Torpey and Adie Orr for the 2005/6 season.

For the 2006/7 season, Sam Ashton made 50 appearances (40 league and 10 cup games) with Stuart Rudd making 49 league and cup appearances with one appearance as a sub.

Extra Time: Nelson FC forced FC United into extra time in their Division Two Cup encounter on 4th February 2006. It was revenge for Nelson, who had lost home and away in the league, as they won 1-0 with a goal in the dying seconds of the second half of extra time. It was the first and last time FC United had to endure extra time in their inaugural season.

Football Club United of Manchester
Created from despair - Powered by passion

F

FA: The club 'FC United of Manchester' was registered as a bona fide football club with the Manchester County Football Association on 14th June 2005.

FA Cup: Registered too late for inclusion, but will be eligible for the 2007/8 season.

FA Vase: The club registered too late to play in the FA Vase for the 2005/6 season, but will be eligible for the 2006/07 season. FC United were given a bye in the first qualifying round and went on to play Brodsworth Minors Welfare in the 2nd qualifying round. FC United went on to win 3-1, with Stuart Rudd, a pre-season signing, scoring FC United's first campaign goal.

Having qualified for the competition proper, FC United faced an old foe, Padiham FC, who were FC United's first ever opponents in a home game.

FC United won 3-0, through Carden (2) and Rudd.

FC United finally fell in the 3rd round to Quorn FC, 2-3.

Families: The Mitten boys (Jonathan and Paul) are cousins, and are related to the legendary Charlie Mitten, who played for Manchester United as a 'Busby Babe'.

FC United of Manchester: The postal address is:

FC UNITED,
ROOM 221, DUCIE HOUSE,
37, DUCIE STREET,
MANCHESTER.
M1 2JW.

In March 2006, FC United moved into larger offices, fortunately in the same building. Two more members of staff were advertised for and the room was needed. The original office was in Room 104.

Fans voted in favour of FCUoM becoming an Industrial and Provident Society, where every member who has pledged any money, regardless of the amount, has one vote. The Board is elected and any profit is ploughed directly back into the club. Those who did pledge money were then asked to vote on the name. The name FC United had originally been put forward, but the FA had rejected it as being too generic. So they were asked to choose from FC United of Manchester, FC Manchester Central, AFC Manchester 1878 and Newton Heath United FC. On 14 June 2005, it was announced that FC United of Manchester had been chosen with 44% of the vote.

Final: FC United played in their first ever cup final on 3rd May 2007.

They reached the final of the League Challenge Cup at the expense of Congleton, who they beat 6-5 over a two-legged semi-final. They met Curzon Ashton FC at Curzon Ashton's home ground and won 2-1.

Football Club United of Manchester

Created from despair - Powered by passion

Fleury, Craig (Midfielder): Born 25/5/1976 in Stockton.

Craig has previously played for Ashton United FC, Cheadle Town, Warrington Town, Salford City and Woodley Sports. A midfielder who scores more than his fair share of goals, he joined Ashton United in 2002 before leaving in February 2005, having moved across town from neighbouring Curzon Ashton. He signed for FC United from Radcliffe Borough FC. He appeared in the first league game against Leek CSOB before FC United's first number seven moved on and joined Offerton Villa, then UniBond Premier side Witton Albion in February 2006.

Formation: Karl Marginson normally favours a 4-4-2 formation, but occasionally deploys a 3-5-2 formation or a 4-3-3 formation, as he did against New Mills. He did employ the 'Christmas Tree' formation 4-3-2-1 in the second half against Ashton Town.

Foster, Liam (Defender): Born 4/9/1987 in Salford.

Reserve Squad.

An exceptional defender who began playing football properly when he was 13, playing for local youth side Deane; and he had a host of top clubs chasing him for trials. Sides like Manchester United and City, Blackburn Rovers Bolton and Crewe offered him trials.

As a Manchester United fan he was over the moon to be asked for a trial at Old Trafford; however, nothing came of it and he spent 18 months at rivals Manchester City. Liam was picked up by Stockport County after impressing in a friendly game between Deane and Stockport County.

Liam came through the Stockport County Youth Academy and made his debut as a substitute in the home loss to Lincoln City in February 2006. During his time at Stockport County he gained a Diploma in Sports Studies whilst continuing to impress during the 2004/5 seasons, but unfortunately he was released in May 2006.

Despite the rejection and having had time to reflect, Darren Lyons noted the availability of the mega-talented youngster and invited him to FC for training.

Liam enjoyed the atmosphere and the set-up so much he stayed. Liam played in the pre-season friendly against Kirkham and Wesham in July 2006.

Liam made his debut in the 3-2 home win over Ramsbottom United AFC in December 2006 and was soon on the score sheet as he put the ball into his own net, giving the visitors a 2-0 lead. Liam came up through FC United's reserve team.

Founded: The club was officially founded on 14th June 2005.

Fox, Matt: Assistant physiotherapist.

Friendlies: FC United did play a number of friendly games against lesser-known local clubs before the first official friendly against Leigh RMI on 16th July 2006. Over 2,550 people turned up to see history in the making as FC United and Leigh RMI entertained the crowd to a hard-fought nil-nil draw. FC United went on to play friendlies against AFC Wimbledon, losing 1-0 in the Direct Supporters Cup and 2-0 against Stalybridge Celtic in a game dedicated to Myra Mandryk, who was seriously ill.

FC Lokomotive Leipzig, a German fan-owned club, reputedly the world's best supported non-league club, invited FC United to play a friendly in Germany on 12th May 2006. The game ended in a 4-4 draw.

The first friendly against their hosts, however, didn't come about until after the end of their inaugural season on Wednesday 19th July 2006.

G

Galway United FC: The only club in Ireland to have a Supporters Trust. The Trust had grown in strength and managed to get a Seat on the Board and were keen to build relationships with other clubs such as FC United. The Trust had arranged a pre-season trip to the UK and invited to play in a pre-season friendly behind closed doors in February. As the game gave manager Karl Marginson a chance to see some of the fringe players in action, the invitation was accepted. There was some discussion over this fixture, as the General Manager of Galway United FC is Nick Leeson, a former employee of Barings Bank. FC United's policy is to support football clubs who are actively encouraging supporter involvement, but unfortunately the game was called off as FC United had too many injuries!

Gates: For the league and cup games in 2005/6 season, 103,075 fans have passed through the turnstiles and seen the phenomenon that is FC United, averaging 3,059 per game.

George, Barrie (Goalkeeper): Born 10/4/1986 in Manchester.

Barrie was a teenager at Altrincham. He was the reserve and youth team keeper for the seasons 2002/3 and 2003/4. He also made 8 appearances for Cheshire FA. He signed UniBond forms at the end of March 2004. He moved to Radcliffe Borough in the summer of 2004, before signing for FCUoM in July 2005, although he almost signed for Leigh RMI. Barrie has also kept goal for the England Partially-Sighted XI as the team's fully-sighted goalkeeper. Barrie was voted 'Man of the Match' against AFC Wimbledon in the Supporters Cup.

Left FC United in search of regular first team football in September 2006 and joined rivals Salford City FC.

Giggs, Rhodri (Striker): Born 2/4/1977 in Cardiff.

One of life's more colourful characters, Rhodri preferred rugby to football, inspired by his father, who was a rugby union player at Swinton. It was only at school when he discovered that rugby was becoming harder and faster but he wasn't growing physically to cope with the demands of the sport. So he started playing more football and earned himself a place in the school side, playing up front or on the right wing due to his speed.

The teenage Giggs impressed his teachers so much that he was recommended to play for Salford Boys, a feat that amused him as he was still playing rugby for Salford! At this stage, Giggs was not looking to football as a career until Division Two side Torquay United came to see the exceptional skills of the young Giggs and offered him a two-year Youth Training Scheme (YTS) contract miles from home. Rhodri took the offer and moved into digs and worked hard at making a go at football. His devotion and dedication earned him rapid progress through the youth and reserve sides, breaking into the first team aged just 16. Rhodri used the name Jones to hide his brother's identity and to be treated as a normal player.

Unfortunately, he only played a few times before he left the club mid-YTS and returned to Manchester and quit football for three years. When the urge to play again returned, he took his skills to Scotland, where he had trials with Hearts which came to nothing; but at Livingston he stayed for 6 months before deciding that he wasn't earning enough playing football to pay the bills, so he took up a job in London, not playing football again for another three years.

After a while, Rhodri moved back to Manchester and his desire to play football returned, joining Welsh side Bangor City in October 2000. At Bangor he played alongside Clayton Blackmore under then manager Peter Davenport, both ex-Manchester United, and briefly playing for Aberystwyth Town.

Salford City were enjoying a good season and close to promotion; Rhodri was enjoying his football and earning respect from his team mates, players such as Karl Marginson, Dave Brown, Phil Melville and Tony Cullen, all of whom he would team up with later. Whilst at Salford City he had a trial with Hereford United but to no avail and then a spell at Kidsgrove Athletic before settling at Bacup Borough in October 2003, making his home debut in the October. He stayed for the remainder of the season, joining Mossley in February 2004.

It was at Mossley that Rhodri really came into his own, with many of the national tabloids drawing a comparison between him and his older brother Ryan. He helped Mossley close in on certain promotion only for them to be deducted 6 points by the league and the hard-earned promotion was denied them.

In his second season there he was awarded the supporters' 'Player of the Year' award and the Dennis Cawthorne Memorial Trophy.

A change of management in the following season saw Giggs leave the club.

Rhodri starred in a celebrity team playing a charity match for injured rugby player Chris McGuirk against FC United and he continued to impress Karl Marginson, who invited him for trials and subsequent pre-season training.

Rhodri earned himself a place in the squad, playing in a pre-season friendly against Radcliffe Borough and then in the Supporters Direct Cup game, a game that saw FC United gain revenge for last season's defeat.

Rhodri went on to make his league debut against St Helen's Town in August 2006, but it wasn't until the end of August that this mega-talented striker scored his first goals with a brace against Flixton FC in a 4-0 win. He celebrated his first goal for the club by running over to the fans and falling on his bum! Giggs played in the FA Vase qualifying rounds and the competition proper against Padiham and has also been in the cup side vying for the Football League Challenge Cup, where he scored in the 3-0 win over Nantwich Town.

Football Club United of Manchester

Created from despair - Powered by passion

Rhodri Giggs

Gilligan, Ryan (Central Midfield): Born 26/9/1979 in Manchester.

Signed from Flixton FC and has played for Altrincham. Due to increased competition, Ryan couldn't be guaranteed a regular starting place, and whilst that is every manager's dream, it is a nightmare for the players concerned. Ryan was in the squad to play against AFC Wimbledon for the Supporters Direct Cup. Ryan left the club at the beginning of December to play regular football and re-signed for Flixton. Ryan appeared in the side that inflicted the second home defeat to FC United.

Goals:

Bizarre: The most bizarre goal came during the 4-0 away win against Ashton Town. The ball was kicked upfield by the FC United back line into Ashton's half. Both Phil Power and Rory Patterson were retreating from an off-side position and the ball flew over their heads towards Ashton's corner flag. Neither player chased the ball and the linesman flagged for off-side. Ashton's goalkeeper, Danny Vickers, threw the ball towards Patterson for the free kick and a stunned Patterson gratefully accepted the ball, rounded the astonished Vickers to score. Vickers hadn't realised the referee had waved play on!

Consecutive: Simon Carden scored in five consecutive league and cup games, amassing 11 goals in the process.

FCUoM scored in an incredible 11 consecutive league games, 12 if you include the League Challenge Cup game.

Disallowed Goals: FCUoM's first disallowed goal came in the 4th minute of FC United's home victory against Eccleshall,: Rob Nugent headed in Steve Torpey's cross, only for the referee to disallow the goal for offside. In the second half, Joz Mitten also had a goal disallowed.

In the 6-0 home victory over Daisy Hill, both sides had goals disallowed, but Joz Mitten had 2 efforts ruled out.

Fastest Cup Goal: Simon Carden scored on eight minutes in the 5-0 win over New Mills in the 2nd round of the Division Two Trophy on 3rd December, having been set up by the eventual man of the match Steve Torpey.

Fastest League Goal: Scored by Simon Carden in 30 seconds in the 10-2 home victory over Castleton Gabriels.

Friendlies: The first goal in a friendly game was scored by Steve Torpey. After going 3 games (281 minutes) without scoring, Torpey scored against Flixton FC, opening the floodgates as FCUoM won 5-2.

Football Club United of Manchester
Created from despair - Powered by passion

Individual: Simon Carden has the best individual performance: he scored 5 in the 10 – 2 home victory against Castleton Gabriels in December.

League: The first league goal in a home game went to Rory Patterson in a 3-2 win against Padiham.

Steve Spencer has the honour of scoring the first away league goal against Leek CSOB in a 2-5 victory.

League Goals – Most: FC United's goal tally for the season 2006/7 was 135, bettering the previous season's tally of 111. **Least**: In the 2005/6 season, FC United conceded 35 goals.

Most Cup Goals: In the two cup competitions Steve Torpey scored 4 cup goals, 3 in the Division Two Cup and 1 on the League Challenge Cup. In the 2006/7 season Stuart Rudd scored 7 goals, 3 in the FA Vase and 4 in the League Challenge Cup.

Most Goals in a Match: The most goals scored in a league game are 10 in the 10-2 home win against Castleton Gabriels on 10th December 2005. Simon Carden scored 5, Joz Mitten a brace and one each for Orr, Torpey and Howard.

Own Goals: No-one has scored a league own goal during the 2005/06 season, though Steve Spencer was unfortunate to score an own goal in the 2-0 defeat in the Stalybridge friendly and Rob Nugent was unfortunate to score the club's first own goal overseas in the 4-4 draw with Lokomotive Leipzig.

Season Total: The highest number of goals scored by an FC United player in all competitions during their inaugural season is 19 by Rory Patterson. Stuart Rudd scored 45 goals in the 2006/7 season, 38 league, 3 in the FA Vase and 4 in the League Challenge Cup.

Green, Adam:

Adam was named in the squad for the friendly against Kirkham and Wesham in July 2006.

Greenhalgh, Lawrence (Assistant Manager): Born 2/4/1974 in Salford.

Loz played at respected side Salford Boys U11s and equally renowned Sunday side Barr Hill, such was his talent, eventually signing pro forms with Bury. Later, he had a brief stint at Leigh RMI, but joined Radcliffe Borough in 1996, making his debut in the same year. He and Tony Cullen were team mates and an unfortunate assault saw Loz have his jaw broken, having been punched by a defender, and Tony took him to hospital.

He joined Salford City and had a couple of injuries, which saw him leave in March 2003, joining Monton Amateurs, where he stayed until 2004.

He had spells with Stalybridge Celtic, Warrington Town and Rossendale before retiring due to injuries. Tony Cullen had also retired from football to coach and saw Loz as an ideal coach, and he was appointed assistant manager of the reserve side for the 2006/07 season on 5th April 2006.

Grimsby Town: League Division Two side Grimsby Town were the first league club to take on trial a player registered with FC United. Will Ahern had a trial with the Mariners on Wednesday 22nd March 2006 and played for their reserves against York City. The following week the Mariners took both Will Ahern and Rory

Football Club United of Manchester
Created from despair - Powered by passion

Patterson on trial. Assistant manager Graham Rodger was so impressed that the duo were invited back the following week. Although no decision had been taken as to whether they would be signed up, the club was aware that scouts from other clubs were at the games watching the boys.

Karl Marginson, who went and watched the lads play at Grimsby, said, "The Grimsby assistant manager said both of them acquitted themselves well. Will plays with great maturity for a 19-year-old and is a real players' player; while Rory has now got his head sorted after the hard knock of being released by Rochdale after being their Young Player of the Year."

Ground: The address is:

Gigg Lane,

Bury,

Lancashire,

BL9 9HR. Gigg Lane is the home of Bury Football Club. It was founded in 1885, though new stands were added in the beginning of 1993. The pitch measures 112 x 73 yards and has a capacity of 11,840. FCUoM will ground share with Bury FC for one year.

H

Hardy, Matt (Midfielder):

Matt featured in one game against Winsford United FC in August 2005, listed as substitute in the 2-2 draw.

Harrop, Kyle (Midfielder): Born 22/4/87.

Reserve Squad.

An inspirational midfielder with a great eye for goal and played a large part in FC United's reserve team success. He played in the reserve game against Warrington Town Reserves in August 2006 and scored a goal in the 4-1 win in the Reserve Cup final against Padiham.

He was on the bench for the 1st team in the hard-fought 1-1 draw away to Nantwich Town, but was not used.

Hat-trick: Darren 'Daz' Lyons scored the club's first hat-trick in a friendly game against Flixton FC. The first competitive hat-trick belongs to Adie Orr. He scored the magic 3 in a cup game away to Cheadle Town on 17th October 2005. The honour of scoring the first hat-trick in a home league game belongs to Simon Carden, who scored with two first half strikes and a goal early in the second half against New Mills FC on 23rd November 2005. The 18-minute burst ensured his name went into the record books.

Rory Patterson, the scorer of many wonderful goals, produced two consecutive hat-tricks. He scored against Trafford and Formby in the last two home games of the 2006/7 season.

Other hat-tricks include having attendances of over 3,000 for 3 home league games in a row.: 3,110 at home to Oldham, 3,808 against Daisy Hill and 3,093 at home to Nelson. Another hat-trick is scoring 5 or more goals 3 games consecutively. Six goals were scored against Daisy Hill, five against Cheadle Town and Nelson.

Football Club United of Manchester

Created from despair - Powered by passion

Hayden, George (Kit man):

This 41-year-old Sergeant-Major is a warrant officer in the British Army with 24 years' service and moonlights as the kit man for FCUoM on match days. He has to his credit an MBE medal for Distinguished Military Conduct. A staunch Manchester United fan and season ticket holder for many years, he stopped renewing his ticket when the prices became too high. A qualified FA coach, he has arranged many overseas football tours in the past for professional clubs such as Bolton Wanderers and Oldham Athletic. Since the takeover, he has made FCUoM his job. Part of George's 'duties' include laying out the kits, making tea, looking after the ball boys, and catering to the whims of the team. Currently, FCUoM have one home and one away strip.

Hayley, Matt (Midfielder): Born 2/11/1985 in Manchester.

Once on the books of Blackburn County, Matt came through the trials playing in 3 pre-season friendlies. He played against Stalybridge Celtic on 30th July 2005 and Flixton FC on 2nd August 2005 and Matt was listed in the squad for FC United's first ever friendly game against Leigh RMI, as well as being in the squad to play AFC Wimbledon in the Supporters Direct Cup. He was selected for the league game against Blackpool Mechanics as a substitute. He became the second player to leave FCUoM in search of regular football, joining Flixton FC during September 2005.

Heaviest Defeat: The heaviest defeat inflicted on FC United was 3-0 by Atherton Collieries on 29th November 2006 in the 2006/7 season.

Until then, 2-1 had been the heaviest defeat inflicted on FC United and this happened twice in their first season. The first was by Norton United at home on 24th September 2005 and the second by Flixton on 15th March 2006. FC United did lose 2-1 to Colne in the NWC Division Two Challenge Cup in November 2005.

Hevicon, Ryan (Left winger): Born 3/11/1982 in Manchester. Signed for FCUoM in July 2005. Signed from Trafford FC, having spent time coming through the youth scheme at Blackburn Rovers, before moving on to Altrincham, Carlisle and Hyde United. He played in a pre-season friendly against Leigh RMI, and was listed in the squad to face AFC Wimbledon for the Supporters Direct Cup before joining Chadderton FC in August 2005.

Hevingham, Aaron (Midfield):
Aaron was in Altrincham's youth set-up for the 2002/03, and for the 2004/05 season he joined Wythenshawe Town. He attended the trials held in the June and in the July of 2005 he was enjoying playing for FC United and was listed in the squad for the Supporters Direct Cup against AFC Wimbledon. He left FC United in search of regular football, moving to Flixton.

Higgins, Matthew (Goalkeeper): Born 17/10/1984 in Macclesfield.

Matt was the first signing of 2006, agreeing to join on 6th January. This highly-rated goalkeeper joined his boyhood team Macclesfield as a trainee in July 2001 and was released in June 2004. He had a month's loan at Nationwide North side Vauxhall

Motors in November 2003, making his debut in an impressive 1-1 draw with Runcorn. Matt had spells with Middlewich Town and Nantwich Town in July and September 2004 before leaving for America to play football. Matt was listed in the squad to face Blackpool Mechanics in September 2005.

History: The idea of forming a new football club had been mooted during the fight against Rupert Murdoch when he tried unsuccessfully to take over Manchester United. The idea of a new club was thought to be too radical. The formation of the club took on more credibility during the fight with Malcolm Glazer, and although the supporters had their own reasons for wanting the new club, Glazer's unwanted takeover was the catalyst behind it. The new club was formed in the summer of 2005. During a Manchester United supporters' meeting on 19th May 2005, Andy Walsh, the chairman, announced that a second meeting would be taking place at the Apollo Theatre on 30th May to discuss further the new club. It was also announced that Kris Stewart, the chairman of AFC Wimbledon, had given advice on forming a new club. AFC Wimbledon is another supporter-owned club. Stewart was to address a subsequent meeting and offered AFC Wimbledon's support. The club was accepted into the North West Counties League in June 2005. There were 4 spaces available in the division and so no teams were rejected because of FC United's application. The North West Counties Football League is on level 10 in the English football league system, 9 levels lower than the English Premier League.

Holt, Scott (Right midfield): Born 22/3/1983 in Manchester. Scott played for his insurance company, the Co-operative

Insurance Company (CIS) in a UK-wide tournament and helped his side to the All Insurance Cup Final at Villa Park against an American insurance company based in the UK.

He scored in every round except the final.

Played for Failsworth Town in the Manchester Challenge Cup in 2001 and East Manchester in 2003, where he teamed up with Darren Lyons, who was to play a part in his career. Scott was unavailable to play Saturdays, but as soon as he became free, Daz Lyons took him to Salford City in the 2004/5 season. Scott continued scoring goals regularly but Daz moved on and, unfortunately for Scott, he picked up a red card playing for his Sunday side which affected the Saturday fixtures as well. Alas, Scott forgot to inform his new boss, ex-Manchester City player John Foster, who dropped him, despite still scoring goals at a rate of one a game. The red card was appealed and rescinded and Scott decided to leave. He was pointed in the direction of Martin Iverson, the manager at Chadderton FC, who were struggling, and Scott scored twice on his debut in a 2-2 draw. Scott went on to score 14 goals in the last ten games of the season, including the winner over Karl Marginson's Flixton on the last day of the season, ensuring his side leapfrogged over Flixton to finish third from bottom. Scott heard about the forming of a new club over the summer and player/coach Daz Lyons knew of his scoring ability and called him up and invited him to pre-season training. Scott believed in the principle behind FC United and enjoyed the spirit and the noise the fans made, so he joined up. Scott played in the first friendly against Leigh RMI and in the Supporters Cup game against AFC Wimbledon. Sadly, he was injured for the first few league games, but played at Northwich Victoria against Ashton Town, where he scored twice. Injury meant that he had to fight to regain his place in a successful side and he went out on loan to Glossop North End in November. He was recalled in the January, but allowed to leave shortly after.

Home Wins: During the inaugural season, FC United won 11 games at home.

During the 2006/7 season FC United won 19 home games.

Home Losses: FC United's impressive opening season ended with just the one home loss.

This feat was mirrored in the 2006/7 season with just the one home loss – shame it was the club's biggest defeat: 3-0.

Honours:

North West Counties Football League Division Two title 2005/6.

Winners of the Supporters Direct Cup 2006/7.

North West Counties Football League Division One title 2006/7.

NWCF League Challenge Cup 2006/7.

Howard, Joshua (Midfield): Born 15/11/1980 in Ashton-under-Lyne, Manchester.

FC United were delighted to sign Joshua; he joined FCUoM from Mossley and made his debut in the cup game against Colne. He graduated through the junior ranks at Old Trafford, where he made 22 appearances and captained the reserve team which included John O'Shea, Luke Chadwick and Michael Stewart. Joshua left Old Trafford after signing for another football agent and moved to Preston North End. Unfortunately, it didn't work out and he joined Stockport County. A spell at Bristol Rovers ended when the club were experiencing financial difficulties and couldn't offer him a contract. Having left Bristol, Joshua trained with Rotherham United, earning himself a call-up with Stalybridge Celtic in December 2000. A brief spell at Hyde United in October 2001 and then Barnet before retiring from the game, disillusioned. It was through an ex-Manchester United player, Lee Martin, that Joshua was contacted by Mossley and his love of football was rekindled. He joined Mossley in the summer of 2002. Unfortunately, a shoulder injury kept him out for a large part of the season. During his last full season at Mossley, however, he chipped in with an excellent tally of 13 goals, which helped gain Mossley promotion to the Unibond League. He went on to make 122 appearances, scoring 24 goals, became their captain and helped them to win their first trophy for 12 years. Joshua has his sights set on being the first international to play for FC United. It was during his Mossley period that it was discovered that Joshua's grandfather was born in Guyana. Joshua was invited to play for Guyana but had to decline because of an injury, although he is due to meet up with officials from Guyana to discuss his debut. Guyana plays in the North and Central American and Caribbean Zone. Joshua is now studying at Manchester Metropolitan University. He is a tough midfielder with remarkable vision for finding his colleagues and the net, as his goal against Darwen proved when he scored from the half-way line, catching the keeper off his line.

Josh scored the winner with an individual display of genius as he helped FC United win the NWCFL Challenge Cup and helping FC complete a league and cup double in the 2006/7 season.

Josh Howard

Internationals: FCUoM have no current international players, but Joshua Howard has set his sights on being the first after it was discovered that his grandfather was born in Guyana.

J

Jean, Wes (Forward):

A much-travelled striker, Wes made his debut at Barton Rovers in September 1999 with a brief spell at Kempston Rovers in the October before returning to Barton. In September 2003 he joined Potton United, staying there until August 2004. In the July of 2005 he appeared for FC United at the Supporters Direct Cup game against AFC Wimbledon, but in the August he moved to Monton Amateurs.

K

Kick-off: The kick-offs for a number of games were delayed due to the large size of the crowd. Most clubs at this level average 65 to 100 per game, but FC United's fans number thousands and the ground staff have worked very hard at the grounds to ensure that the crowds are safely in. Even the League Challenge Cup game against Cheadle Town was subject to delay.

Kit: FC United encountered technical difficulties prior to the historic meeting between Leigh RMI and FC United. The difficulty: a clash of strips because FC United only had a home outfit! FC United wouldn't have an away strip ready in time to play and Leigh stepped in to help. They arranged with their suppliers to receive an old away kit, remove the logos, replace them with the new ones and send them back in double quick time. This enabled FC United to play in their traditional red, white and black with Leigh in yellow.

Kit Aid: Set up in 1998 and organised by Three Valleys Water Company Plc to send football kits overseas to third world countries. To date, Kit Aid have sent over 10,000 shirts and FC United held a Kit Aid day on 22nd April 2006 for the home game against Great Harwood Town FC.

Krupa, Jan (Reserve team kit man and physiotherapist).

L

League Points: In the inaugural season, FC United amassed 87 points, coming from 27 wins, 6 draws and 3 losses in 36 games. FC United finished the 2006/7 season with a record number of points for the club: 112.

Leek CSOB FC: The first ever league game played by FC United was away to Leek CSOB. Formed in 1945 by the late schoolmaster Trevor Harvey to provide football and other sports for the youngsters leaving school at the end of WWII, Leek started off in the local youth leagues and entered senior football in 1959/60 season when they joined the Leek and Moorland League, winning the Leek Post Charity Shield. Over the following years the club enjoyed success in winning trophies, including the coveted Sentinel Cup, promotion, League Cups, Championship and League Cup doubles, and gaining promotion to the North West Counties Football League Division Two in 1995/96, when they also won League Cup, League Shield, the Leek Shield, and the whole squad represented the league in the Inter-League Cup, winning against a Liverpool League Representative side.

Leek were promoted to the NWCFL Division 1 in the 1997/98 season, where they remained for a number of seasons before being relegated. Leek CSOB have never had a ground of their own and have had to hire grounds before a generous benefactor donated £300,000 to the club for the sole purpose of developing a stadium with training facilities. Leek are currently negotiating with the necessary governing bodies to build the stadium in a project known as 'The Birchall Community Re-Generation Project'. The club gained the 'FA Charter Standard Community Development Club' status; amazing, since the club does not have a base. Colin Fletcher of Leek CSOB scored the first goal against FC United after 14 minutes in the 2-5 home defeat.

Leigh RMI: History was made when FC United played Leigh RMI in a friendly game on Saturday 16th July 2005. It heralded the beginning of a new football club and how pertinent that it should be against the club that had been discussed as a takeover. Both teams come from similar backgrounds, having links with the railways and body repair workshops. The RMI stands for Railway Mechanics Institute. Founded in 1896 and known as Horwich RMI FC until 1995 when the club, realising the need to improve their status and move up the football pyramid, moved to their new ground at Hilton Park in Leigh. Once the move had been

Football Club United of Manchester
Created from despair - Powered by passion

finalised, Horwich officially changed their name to reflect their new surroundings. Leigh RMI reached the pinnacle of their career when they achieved promotion to the Conference, where they enjoyed a lengthy spell, but because of their second bottom finish in the 2003/04 season, they were to be relegated to the new Conference North Division for the 2004/05 season. However, they were spared relegation that season due to the lack of promotable Northern Premier League clubs and Margate were then demoted because their ground failed to meet safety standards. This reprieve only lasted one season, as they finished bottom in 2004/05. The club is planning to relocate to a new purpose-built stadium.

Lokomotivee Leipzig FC: Originally formed in 1896 as VFB Leipzig, Lokomotivee was one of the 86 teams that came together in the city in 1900 to form the German Football Association and wrote history when they won the first National Championship in 1903.

In the period leading up to WWII, VFB Leipzig were unable to repeat their earlier success. The league was re-structured under the Third Reich in 1933 and although they enjoyed success in their new division they were unable to progress further.

After the war the club was disbanded under the occupying Allied Forces. The club was re-constituted by club members in 1946 as SG Probstheida, under the auspices of the occupying Russian forces. The team played under the names BSG Erichzeigner Probstheida and BSG Einhart Ost before being merged with SC Rotation Leipzig in 1954 and playing in Germany's top flight.

In 1963, Leipzig's two most important clubs – SC Rotation and SC Lokomotive Leipzig – were placed together and two new teams were created, SC Leipzig and BSG Chemie Leipzig. Another re-organisation in 1965 saw SC Leipzig become FC Lokomotive Leipzig and BSG Chemie Leipzig take on a company name. It was at this time that the club became a 'Stasi-club', where players from Chemie were forced by the state to play for rival clubs.

Despite this, BSG Chemie Leipzig went on to win the title in 1963/64 season.

In Leipzig this is still known as the 'Leutzscher Legende' (The Legend of Leutzscher, after the city part of Chemie).

Playing as FC Lokomotive Leipzig (LOK), the club's fortunes improved, but they were still unable to win the title.

LOK won a host of East German Cups and the EUFA Intertoto Cup in 1966 and were the losing side in the 1987 EUFA Cup Winners Cup.

Re-unification in 1990 was followed by the merger of the two football leagues of the two countries. The club changed names by reclaiming the title VFB Leipzig in an attempt to re-ignite their fortunes after a poor season, and a third-placed finish saw the club promoted to the Bundesliga. Unfortunately, the following season they finished joint last and a long slide began: relegation to the Regionalliga NordOst (III) then down to the Oberliga NordOst/Sud (IV) by 2001. From there it went from bad to worse as the club was declared bankrupt in 2004, their results being annulled and the club dissolved.

The club was reborn in 2004 by the fans as FC Lokomotive Leipzig and, like FC United, began life in the lower echelons of the league set-up in the 11th tier Kreisklasse Staffel 2 in the 2004/5 season.

Continued solid support from the fans ensured financial security

Football Club United of Manchester
Created from despair - Powered by passion

and the club went on to break the world record for lower league attendances, with 12,421 fans watching them play Eintracht Grossdeubens second team on 9th October 2004. The club merged with SSV Torgau in 2005/6 and now play in the 7th tier Bezirksklasse Leipzig Staffel 2.

It is reputed to be the world's largest non-league football club.

Lomax, Mike (Defender): Born 7/12/1979 in Whitington.

Mike played in a pre-season friendly against Sheffield FC on 29th July 2006. He made his first team debut on 30th August 2006 against Flixton, earning himself a yellow card in the 4-0 win. He also came on as a sub in the FA Vase game against Padiham in the October that year. He was impressive in the 7-0 win over Stone Dominoes and equally impressive in the 7-1 win over Abbey Hey, which was his last game in an FC United shirt. Left the club 2006/7 season and joined Winsford United.

Previous clubs: Blackburn Rovers, Macclesfield Town, Castle Utd (Singapore) Marine, Hyde Utd, Trafford and Salford City.

Lost Balls: It took the very talented Adie Orr just 41 minutes to lose the first football of the season. During the first home game against Padiham he kicked the ball onto the roof of Gigg Lane to rapturous applause from the Manchester Road End. A change of ball was used in the Castleton Gabriels game after the FC United number 4 blasted it high and wide.

Lyons, Darren (Forward/player coach): Born 9/11/1965 in Manchester.

Nicknamed 'Daz', Darren was signed for his vast experience. He started his playing career at Oldham Athletic in the early 1980s.

After Rhyl and Droylsden, he had a trial at Derby County before Leek Town (1990/01). Darren then joined Mossley for £500, then to Accrington Stanley for £500, before joining Bury. Having joined 3rd Division outfit Bury in March 1992, he scored 4 goals in 10 appearances and then signed professional forms before playing 26 more times. He was transferred for a £3,000 fee to Southport County, but left in December 2003. Daz moved to Macclesfield Town and joined Sammy McIlroy's success story until August 1996. He then had a brief stop at Salford City before another £3,000 transfer to Halifax Town and helping them to Nationwide Conference promotion. 16 appearances for Morecambe followed during the 1999/00 season, debuting in October 1999. Later, he returned to Southport County for the 2000/01 season, making another debut in March 2000. Daz was made player/manager of East Manchester in August 2003 before moving back to Salford City in July 2003 and where he was again made manager in September, making 45 appearances. Darren announced his availability to the North West Counties Football League in March 2005, and then in April 2005 he left to join Ashford United before a very brief spell at Flixton and finally FC United. A player for the big occasion, he has played in front of 55,000 fans at Old Trafford against Manchester United legend Eric Cantona. He was a member of the original squad who eventually retired from the game at the end of the 2006/7 season having helped FC United gain promotion to the UniBond Northern Premier League and playing in the last home game of the season against Formby in the 5-0 win.

M

Man of the Match: The first man of the match was Adie Orr in

Football Club United of Manchester
Created from despair - Powered by passion

the home game against Padiham, as chosen by the match sponsors Tempest Sports.

Manager: The current manager is Karl Marginson. He was chosen in June 2005 for his vast experience at both league and non-league football, having been nominated by Joz Mitten.

Manager of the Month: Karl won this prestigious award three times in Division Two.   He was deservedly awarded his first 'Manager of the Month' award for the month of October 2005 before the home game against New Mills.

He then collected the award in December 2005 and for the third time in March 2006.

He was awarded the managerial prize in September 2006, February 2007 and again in March 2007 for Division One.

Manager of the Year: Karl Marginson was voted 'Division One Manager of the Year' in June 2007.

Marginson, Karl (Manager): Born 11/11/1970 in Manchester.

A born winner! Karl earned his place in both his primary and junior school teams and at weekends he turned out for Newbury Aces in order to gain more experience. But it was some of the other boys who were invited for trials instead – not that it stopped him from attending the trials, such was his confidence – and he stayed there until he was 15 or 16. Again, Karl wasn't counting on football to pay his way and he took on a job outside football just in case. Alas, it was this back-up plan that worked against him because the when the YTS contracts were being handed out he wasn't offered one because he already had a job and it wouldn't be fair to the other lads. Karl moved on and managed to get a trial at Bradford City, but again no contract, so he tried Stockport County and he was turned down again. Not that it stopped him from gaining valuable experience playing in the youth side. Then Karl went on to have spells at Tranmere Rovers and Blackpool, making the reserves for both teams and getting to the fringe of breaking into the first team. It was whilst at Blackpool playing in the FA youth side that changed his life. The side were playing badly and the youth team manager, Sam Ellis, slated the team, especially the number four who would never make a footballer as he wasn't physical enough. Karl hadn't realised it was him, but left the club when he found out. Instead of giving up, he did the opposite and joined the toughest team in the league and soon learnt his way round the park!

Brief spells at Curzon Ashton and Droylsden followed before he settled at Ashton United. In fact, he settled down so well that he was soon the attention of scouts and Sam Ellis wanted him to join him at Manchester City, offering the club £5,000. The club turned it down as being inadequate!

Having gained revenge on Ellis, Karl was thoroughly enjoying his football to the extent that he once again caught the attention of the scouts and he very nearly signed for Burnley, but did sign for Rotherham, making his debut three weeks later and he enjoyed regular games until he fell foul of the manager.

Unfortunately for Karl, an injury kept him out of the game at the time his contract was up for renewal and it wasn't renewed.

Not one to be put down, Karl fought his way back to fitness and

Football Club United of Manchester
Created from despair - Powered by passion

joined Macclesfield Town under the guidance of Sammy McIlroy, but he didn't enjoy his football and left after one season, then joining Chorley. Yet another injury saw the midfielder sidelined again, but he regained his fitness and was transferred to Barrow FC for £5,000. He began enjoying his football again and will be remembered for scoring the goal that helped clinch the UniBond title later that year and promotion to the Conference. In all, he spent 3 years at Holker Street, making 78 appearances, and in 1999 it was money matters that interrupted Karl's career and he left the club.

He joined Stalybridge Celtic in February 1999 and the striker hit a rich vein of scoring, hitting the net 11 times in 11 games; but another serious injury left him on the sidelines again. Not for the first time, he fought to regain his fitness and as he was ready to play the club was performing well on the pitch but money was again tight and Karl left the club in the November.

This time he signed for Hyde United and he made his debut in February 2000 in a 4-0 victory over Gainsborough.

An enjoyable 3-year stint at Salford City followed, and so did his first taste of coaching. At the tender age of 27, he began to see football from a different viewpoint and Karl took on various coaching roles; after a period of 2 years and a decent spell at Radcliffe Borough between 2002 and 2004, even getting himself sent off in an FA Vase cup game against Mossley. However, Karl found himself back at Flixton getting more valuable coaching experience.

Karl had heard about FC United and was stunned to be offered the chance to manage the fledgling club after Joz Mitten had told the steering group there was only one man suitable for the job.

Karl signed from Flixton Town FC, where he was the assistant manager. As a player he had vast experience of both league and non-league football and was widely respected as a tough midfielder. His knowledge of playing non-league football in the north-east from his time at clubs such as Salford City, Hyde United, Stalybridge Celtic, Barrow, Chorley, Droylsden and Curzon Ashton, made him the ideal candidate. Karl then spent the 2004/05 season playing for Bacup Borough in the Moore & Co Construction Solicitors League. The new manager was introduced to the football world at 8am on 22nd June 2005: half way through his day's work delivering food to the elderly, Karl donned a suit taken from the back of his fruit and veg van, put money in the meter and then faced the press inside Manchester's historic Midland Hotel, having been appointed manager ahead of stiff competition – such as Sammy McIlroy, Norman Whiteside and Denis Law. Karl had been recommended to the Board by Joz Mitten and he was awarded October's North West Counties Football League 'Manager of the Month', having guided his side to four straight wins, three in the league and one in the League Challenge Cup.

Karl was voted September's 'Manager of the Month' for the first season in the NWCFL Division One. The team played seven and won seven in the opening month of the season.

Despite being the manager and suffering a chronic knee injury, Karl still plays football. He finally hung up his boots coming on as a substitute in the last home game of the 2006/7 season against Formby. He had already guided FC United to a second successive promotion title.

Karl was awarded the 'Division One Manager of the Year' trophy in June 2007.

Football Club United of Manchester

Created from despair - Powered by passion

Karl Marginson

Marksmen: FC United's leading marksman in the 2005/6 season was Rory Patterson, who scored 19 goals in all competitions.

Stuart Rudd, who joined FC United from Skelmersdale prior to the 2006/7 season, continued his rich vein of scoring by hitting the net 45 times in all competitions (38 L, 4 LCC, 3 FAC) in the second season.

Top marksmen in FC history for all competitions:

Rory Patterson 58

Stuart Rudd 45

Simon Carden 34

McCartney, Billy (Defender): Born 16/4/1976 in Manchester.

Like most kids in the area, Billy played football at primary school and even played for a Sunday side (St Thomas More) and, as he progressed through the years, he was made captain of his secondary school side.

His progress had been noted by scouts from Rochdale AFC and he was delighted to sign on schoolboy terms.

As a 17-year-old he was offered a YTS placement at Spotlands and he regarded football as his career.

He worked hard in the youth team in his first year, but his talents really took off in the second. He made the reserve side and eventually captain, but financial constraints on the club meant that none of the YTS players were offered contracts and Billy was released.

Macclesfield Town took Billy on and he played in the reserve side, but after a short while he felt the need to move on. Billy took a job and a few of his mates played for Oldham Town, where he signed up for the 1994/5 season and started to enjoy playing football again.

It was when the manager left that Billy left Oldham and joined Castleton Gabriels and he spent a good couple of seasons there before he joined Ramsbottom United for the 1998/99 seasons.

At Ramsbottom he helped the club make history by qualifying for the FA Cup, beating Maine Road 2-1. Shortly afterwards, he signed for Trafford, after having been approached by them. Ramsbottom United had reported Trafford to the FA over 'illegal' approaches to their players, Billy being one of them.

During his time at Trafford he was voted 'Player of the Year' twice and helped them to win the League Cup. The final was a hard-fought game which went on to be decided by penalties, with Billy scoring the winning penalty.

Billy moved up the UniBond League by joining Stalybridge Celtic in September 2000, but after a short spell he found a new challenge at Salford City and his first encounter with FC United's manager, Karl Marginson, before moving on and joining Chorley for the 2001/1 season. His hard work and no-nonsense attitude earned him the captain's armband and again voted 'Player of the Year' by the fans. He made 49 league and cup appearances in his first season.

As happens at clubs, a change of management came in with different plans and Billy found himself on the move again and in August 2004 he joined Mossley.

Unfortunately, injuries started creeping into his game and he only made a handful of appearances and he left to play for Bacup Borough in October 2004, teaming up with David May and Ben Thornley, both ex-Manchester United players, before leaving in July 2005.

Billy took on a managerial role at Langley Rangers for a short period before again deciding to play football and being connected with Droylsden. It was around this time that Karl Marginson got in touch and offered Billy a part in the FC United club.

He signed for FC United in July 2005 from Droylsden. Billy was FCUoM's first captain and also their first injury. He suffered an elbow dislocation in the very first game against Leigh RMI following an aerial challenge in the first half.

Billy left the club before the start of the 2006/7 season, rejoining Trafford.

Melville, Philip (Goalkeeper): Born 15/1/1973 in Manchester.

Even as a 9-year-old, Phil was bigger than most and used his height and weight advantage to good effect – as a striker!

As a 10-year-old he had a trial with Manchester Boys and spent four years with them, later joining Urmston Boys. He nearly gave up on football when he had a trial with Oldham Athletic against Liverpool Academy and he played badly. His father suggested he try his hand at something else, but a few weeks later the hand of fate turned in his favour. Young Phil was watching a match and one of the sides was short of a keeper and Phil stepped into the breech. As luck would have it, a scout from Manchester City was there and was suitably impressed. Phil was invited for a trial at Maine Road and he managed to get an assistant goalkeeper place, which was quite hard.

Football Club United of Manchester
Created from despair - Powered by passion

On reaching 16, Phil made the decision many schoolboys make and chose football as his career path and he worked hard at developing his skills, attracting the attention of leading clubs; but he accepted a Youth Training Scheme (YTS) placement from Manchester City, the club he followed as a lad.

Even though he was at the club he wanted to join, the opportunity to shine was almost impossible; there were too many goalkeepers and two years wasn't enough time to develop and prove his worth, so he made the decision to transfer his YTS papers to nearby Rotherham United, who had been keeping tabs on the boy. Things didn't work out, so Phil moved to Sheffield United and played against Bristol Rovers, aged 19. He played well in the 0-0 draw and was selected to play in the next game, which they lost 3-2 and Melville wasn't selected again. That was the end of the two years and Phil wasn't offered a contract. Phil tried pastures new and went to Rochdale, but it didn't work out there and Phil took a break from football.

It wasn't long before he craved football again and he joined Radcliffe Borough, where he enjoyed a 3-season spell before he took another break before joining Salford City. At Salford City he met up with future team mates Dave Brown, Rhodri Giggs and Karl Marginson and Salford did well, becoming serious title contenders. Salford City were also losing finalists in the Manchester Premier Cup. Things were looking good when a managerial disagreement meant most of the team walking out of the club, with Phil one of them.

The following season he joined Altrincham briefly before joining Mossley, where he again teamed up with Dave Brown, Rhodri Giggs, Rory Patterson and later Matty Taylor. It was another season of mixed fortunes as Mossley achieved a promotion spot, but an administrative points deduction meant that Mossley weren't promoted.

Another career break followed and Phil came back rejuvenated and re-joined Mossley with FC United in full flow, but a phone call from his old team mate Karl Marginson was enough and Phil signed from Mossley FC as goalkeeping cover after Phil Priestley left the club. In November 2005 he joined Salford City on loan to get match fit and was recalled in January 2006. He left the club in March 2007, joining Division Two outfit Oldham Town.

Merchandise: Club items are for sale on the auction site E-bay and numerous items are for sale on the club's website. Originally, only home shirts were available in two sizes from the site with the embroidered words 'Inaugural Season 2005–2006'.

Mike, Leon (Striker): Born 4/9/1981 in Manchester.

A devoted Manchester United fan trying to emulate his childhood hero Mark Hughes, Leon didn't even own a pair of boots until half an hour before his first game. From then on, his love for the game grew and he turned out for Priory in a junior league. For the next two years Leon plied his trade in midfield with a passion, a passion that was picked up by Trafford Boys. It was here that a scout from Manchester City invited Leon to a trial, but they played him out of position and he picked up an injury. As luck would have it, Manchester City invited him back and this time, in the position of striker, everything fell into place and he signed for them. Manchester United approached him a week later, but he had already committed to their blue rivals.

In fact, Manchester City were so impressed with the talent Leon possessed that they put him forward for a place in the National Sports Centre scheme, a chance to spend two years at a football academy. As a 14-year-old, the option of living away from home and even playing alongside the likes of Wes Brown, Joe Cole and Francis Jeffers still gave Leon cause for concern, but the more he played the more settled in. Eventually, it was decision time for the club, and so highly did they rate Leon that they gave him a three-year Youth Training Scheme (YTS) place instead of the usual two.

Competition for places was tough and, when Leon turned 18, Dennis Smith took him on loan for a month at strugglers Oxford City. Shortly afterwards, Leon was loaned out again, this time to Halifax Town, a team struggling in Division Two; but he was still without a goal. It was the experience gained that allowed Kevin Keegan to extend his stay at Maine Road and he finally got his chance at the expense of an injury to Shaun Goater; but, unfortunately, he still couldn't get on the score sheet. In the January, Leon was sold to Scottish club Aberdeen for £50,000 and he finally broke his duck against Dundee United. After that he began enjoying football properly and goals came by more easily and his exploits meant that Aberdeen qualified for the EUFA Cup. Sadly, 18 months later a change of management meant that the squad changed and Leon began feeling homesick, so he left the club and returned to England in July 2003.

Trials with several English clubs came to nothing and he signed for Mossley in the August. During the 2003/4 season he was Mossley's leading goalscorer, with 18 in all competitions.

Leon was released by Mossley in December 2005 and FC United

were happy to have this former England Youth international in the side. Leon made his debut in the heavyweight fixture against Winsford FC on 2nd January 2006 and unfortunately had a goal disallowed. Leon played 6 times for FC United before leaving the club in January 2007 to play regular football with Flixton and playing alongside former FC United stars Joz Mitten and Ryan Gilligan, who also enjoyed spells at FC United.

Minute's Silence: Sadly, with all clubs there comes a time when it is morally correct to observe a minute's silence for a player or someone who merits our respect and who has passed away. The first such gesture at Gigg Lane for FC United was on 10th September 2005 before the league game with Blackpool Mechanics for Noel Cantwell, a fine and well-respected captain of Manchester United back in the 1960s and who captained the side to FA Cup success in 1963 and who made 144 appearances for Manchester United. Sadly, Noel died on 8th September 2005 after a long illness. At the heart of every FC United fan are the Manchester United stars of yesteryear and the one minute's silence was impeccably observed. Unfortunately, the same cannot be said for the crowd at Old Trafford that day. A minute's silence was also observed before the first home fixture against Padiham for the very tragic death of Nick McCool. The Bury boy was only 20 when he died, playing 5-a-side football in Manchester. He had played for Padiham the season before. Prior to the home game against New Mills, the fans and management paid tribute to Board member and friend Russell Delaney. Instead of a minute's silence, there was a minute of magnificent applause at the referee's whistle in celebration of Russell's life. Sadly, FC United first took part in this tradition at the beginning of the friendly game away to Leigh RMI for the murdered schoolgirl Lauren Pilkington-Smith, who came from

Football Club United of Manchester
Created from despair - Powered by passion

Leigh. Any book relating to a team from Manchester would not be complete without a mention of George Best, probably the greatest footballer to grace the hallowed turf at Old Trafford. It is with heavy heart that only mention in this book celebrates his life as he passed away on Friday 25th November 2005. Football grounds around the country paid their respects to George and FC United were no exception. Playing away to Cheadle Town, both teams celebrated his life by a moment's silence in contemplation followed by a minute's applause.

Mitten, Jonathan (Forward): Born 1/12/1976 in Urmston.

Nicknamed 'Joz' or 'Jozzer', he prefers the latter and is often incorrectly referred to as 'Josh' by the media. Signed for Altrincham in December 2004 and scored on his debut in January 2005 from Ashton United, just as he was about to begin a 3-match ban, which was soon to be followed by a supplementary 5-game ban for the same offence, committed whilst at Ashton. He has appeared for a number of local clubs, including Trafford, Flixton and Curzon Ashton in the 2002/03 season, scoring 17 goals; and played for Radcliffe Borough in 2004. Jonathan was released in late April 2005. Jonathan is the nephew of Altrincham kit man Dave Mitten, who is the brother of sports writer Andy Mitten, and his great uncle was Charlie Mitten, the former Manchester United player and former Altrincham boss. Joz signed for FC United knowing that he was dropping five divisions with a handful of clubs chasing him. He recommended Karl Marginson to the Board. Mr Mitten has the unpleasant record of being the first FC United player to have been cautioned for an over-exuberant goal celebration in the away game at Leek CSOB.

Mitten, Paul (Midfielder): Born 22/12/1975 in Manchester.

Was one of the first to sign for FC United on 8th July 2005 from Abbey Hey FC. Once on Manchester United's books as well as having spent time on the books with Coventry City, Southport County between August 1997 and May 1998, Stalybridge Celtic, Trafford, Ashton Curzon and Mossley. Paul Mitten played with Mossley in the 2002/3 season with Tony Coyne. Paul came on as substitute in the League Challenge Cup game against Cheadle Town. Cousin to Jonathan Mitten and nephew to the great Charlie Mitten, a 'Busby Babe' and in the 1960s the manager of Altrincham.

He only started once for the club, but he will be remembered for his wonderful strike against Nelson.

Due to work and family commitments, Paul left the club in December 2005.

Mortimer, Alex (Defender): Born 28/11/1982 in Trafford.

How this talented left-sided defender managed to slip through the net is beyond belief. Many of the current Premiership and Championship sides had the chance to sign Alex, such is his ability; yet somehow they missed out and FC United reap the rewards.

Alex came to light playing football for his primary school and a scout from Everton invited him to train with Everton's juniors. This arrangement didn't work out and he joined North Trafford Juniors when he was 11. It was while playing for North Trafford Juniors that he was approached by Blackburn Rovers and he had an enjoyable spell at Ewood Park. Such was his enormous talent that Manchester

Football Club United of Manchester
Created from despair - Powered by passion

United came in for him when he was 13 and were so serious about signing him that they arranged a transfer of schools and he finished his education at a school in Ashton. Unfortunately, he saw that the chance of breaking through into the first team was slim, having seen team mate Joshua Howard fall by the wayside, so he decided to move on. At the tender age of 16, he joined Leicester City and so impressed Leicester boss Martin O'Neill that he was offered a six-month Youth Scheme placement, followed by an amazing 4-year professional contract. Soon he was playing regularly for the reserves and this was highlighted when he was selected to play in Martin O'Neill's testimonial game against Celtic and he was given the task of marking Celtic hero Henrik Larsson.

A change in management meant a change of style and again Alex found himself changing clubs. He joined Shrewsbury who, after a bad season, were relegated and Alex became a free agent. He went to Ireland and played for St Patrick FC in a newly-formed league, but soon came home. Back in Manchester, he joined UniBond Premier League side Southport County. He found the strain of employment and training hard work and after 23 appearances for the club he moved on and joined a more local team: Hyde United. Having helped Hyde to promotion, Alex suffered an ankle injury which kept him out of the game for around 5 months. He went out on loan to Flixton, a move made permanent in November 2005. Flixton made him captain and at the time Flixton trailed FC United and Winsford, but Alex helped Flixton to a 12-match unbeaten run as well as taking points off FC United.

Alex wanted a bigger challenge and left Flixton, and a chance meeting between Alex's father and manager Karl Marginson ensured Alex joined FC United, where his enthusiasm and skill has made him a firm favourite with the fans.

Alex Mortimer

Mortimer, Ben (Defender): Born 4/6/85.

Reserve Squad.

Ben didn't come to the attention of the football world until he was 15 and then the top clubs were clambering to get his signature. He had interest from Coventry City but signed for Leicester City, until a serious injury side-lined him.

Ben enjoyed playing with Leicester City Academy U19s, playing against top-flight opposition such as West Ham United, in the 2003/4 season.

Having regained his fitness, he joined FC United, being on the bench for the friendly game against Altrincham. Ben was in the historic side that played in the first ever game for the reserves. The friendly played against Flint Town United was won 1-0 in front of 900 travelling fans. He was also in the friendly game against Kirkham and Wesham in July 2006. His leadership qualities led to manager Tony Cullen giving him the responsibility of the captaincy.

Moore and Co Construction Solicitors: The sponsors name of the North West Counties Football League.

N

National Blood Service: The National Blood Service went to the home game against Leek CSOB on 18th March looking for new recruits and handing out leaflets. Any fan who then went on to donate and handed in the leaflet were entered into a prize draw with the winner receiving a signed shirt.

Newbrook, Dale (Goalkeeper): Born 18/10/82.

Reserve Squad.

As a youngster Dale made the Bolton Boys U14 squad and eventually into the Bolton Boys U15 squad to play in the final of the Greater Manchester Schools Woodhead Cup. He was soon on the books of Altrincham and was their youth team keeper in the 2000/1 season and was a part of the treble-winning side whose trophies included the Bolton and District North West Alliance League and League Cup. He stayed at the club for the 2001/2 season, where his ability and dedication earned him a place in the reserves and eventually he made his debut for the first team in a UniBond League Cup game against Nelson in the October. He went on to be named as substitute goalkeeper for Altrincham manager Graham Heathcote's testimonial match. He went on a short loan spell to BOC Gases before coming back to Altrincham for the remainder of the season and for the 2002/3 season he found himself at Trafford for the first of two visits, playing in the 2nd round of the FA Trophy, until the beginning of the 2004/5 season, where he played for Woodley Sports before joining Leigh RMI's reserves. He was loaned out again, this time to Padiham, but was recalled back to Leigh after an incident and injury left the club short of keepers.

Dale stayed on at Leigh until December 2005 when he left and re-joined Trafford for his second spell and from where he joined FC United in July 2006.

He played in the first ever reserve team match against Flint Town United.

He kept a clean sheet in front of 900 delirious fans and was part of the double-winning side that won the Reserve League and Cup, beating Padiham 4-1 in the final.

Newspapers: FC United have had many match reports in the non-league paper, but they have also had articles in the national broadsheets *Independent* and *Guardian*. Articles have appeared in American, New Zealand, Dutch and Scandinavian magazines and papers as well.

Football Club United of Manchester
Created from despair - Powered by passion

Nickname: Whilst there is no recognised nickname for the club, the terms 'Rebels' and 'Red Rebels' have been used.

Non-Contract: Most of the players are on a non-contract basis. Here a 7-day rule applies. Should a player wish to leave a club, then he hands in a 7-day notice; or, if a club wants a player to leave, they place him on a 7-day notice. Should a player want to leave and has a club willing to take him, then the club can agree to waive the 7-day rule and allow the player to leave early. A club can only place 2 players a month on the 7-day notice. No money changes hands.

Non-League: The *Manchester Evening News* sports writers and journalists who have covered the Premiership, Championship and Football League games have also covered the non-league scene and have voted for the best non-league player of the season. Rory Patterson was amongst the top 10 players nominated and was rated 8/10 by the voters.

North West Counties Football League: This league is also known as the Moore and Co Construction Solicitors League. FCUoM will be playing in the second division of that league for the 2005/6 season. This puts the club at Level 10 of the English football league system, nine levels below the FA Premier League.

The league was founded in 1982 following the amalgamation of the Cheshire County League and Lancashire Combination Leagues. Originally, the League had three divisions, but in 1987 it was reduced to two by the introduction of another level,

Division One into the Northern Premier League and, with some clubs unable to attain the new ground regulations, there were only enough sides for two divisions.

Clitheroe are the only side to have won back-to-back promotions three times, a feat not possible now. Flixton in 1995/96 and Cammell Laird in 2005/6 have both achieved back-to-back promotions, an exclusive club that FC United have now deservedly joined.

Only Ashton United in 1992 and Kidsgrove Athletic in 1998 have achieved a league and cup double, another elite group that FC United have earned the right to join.

Norton United: The first team to defeat FC United at home in a league game, 1-2. Norton United is one of the youngest sides in the North West Counties Football League (NWCFL) and, despite only being 16 years old, they have won 8 trophies. In 1989, Alan Tittensor formed a club in a small town called Smallthorne in Stoke-on-Trent. Alan had realised the potential to start a football club at Norton Cricket Club and Norton United was born. United entered the Staffordshire Senior League and three years later had their first piece of silverware in the form of the Midland League Cup. In 1997 they enjoyed their first double by claiming the Staffordshire Senior League and Cup and in 1999 they won the league title again as well as the Staffordshire FA Senior Vase. Another double followed in 2001 and life in NWCFL Division Two began, and they've remained there ever since. In 2004/5, Norton won the FA Senior Vase for the second time. The grounds and club house have been upgraded and the club has expanded into the community with plans for several teams within the club and already have a second team playing in the Drayton Beaumont Midland League, who are proving to be just as successful as the senior side. Norton United finished 5th last season and have plans to improve upon that this season.

Nugent, Robert (Defender): Born 27/12/1982 in Bolton.

As a youngster, Rob spent time at numerous clubs before Sheffield United showed any sign of interest and it wasn't long before they gave him a Youth Training Scheme (YTS) place. He progressed well through the youth system to the point where he was awarded the captaincy of the reserve side during the 2002/3 season and later he was offered a two year contract and he signed professional forms for the 2002/3 season; unfortunately, he was released in the October by Neil Warnock and joined Ossett Town FC on a free transfer. He struggled to find another Premiership club and trained to become an accountant while continuing to play football on a non-league basis in his spare time.

As a life-long Manchester United fan, he despaired when Glazer's plans became known and as an IMUSA member Rob fought against Glazer, attended the meetings and protested outside Old Trafford. It was his hatred of Glazer and the love of big United that attracted him to the meetings and a subsequent application for trials at FC United. It was at one of these meetings that one of his friends told Luc Zentar about Rob's ability, who passed on his details to Karl Marginson.

He added his name to the list of trial,lists but due to his history he was invited directly to the pre-season friendly, bypassing the need for a trial.

Even though he had been on Ossett Town's books for the past two seasons, he was prepared to play for FCUoM and made his debut in the 0-0 draw versus Leigh RMI. During FC United's initial season he made 30 appearances, scoring four goals in the process; such was his contribution.

Rob was presented with the Manager's 'Player of the Season' award for his enormous contribution during the 2006/7 season.

Rob Nugent

Football Club United of Manchester

Created from despair - Powered by passion

O

Ogden, John (Goalkeeper): Born 17/10/1978.

He spent time at various clubs gaining experience over the years. He joined Ramsbottom United as a 19-year-old and made his debut in March 1998.

In January 2004 he was playing for Heywood Town; in February 2005 he was at Hooley Bridge Celtic, where he stayed until the November, joining Ramsbottom Town before joining Salford City in March 2006. Heywood Reform AFC had his skills from the August and in the October he joined FC United. John was on the subs' bench for the Challenge Cup Final, though he wasn't used.

Oldest Player: The oldest player on FC United's books and to make an appearance was Phil Power; he was 39 years when he scored against New Mills on 3rd December 2005, having come on as a substitute.

O'Neil, Michael (Midfielder):

Reserve Squad.

Michael was signed on 10th February 2006, having played and impressed in a friendly against Glossop North End on Wednesday 8th February. Michael did attend the original trials in June, although he wasn't selected. Mike is listed in the FC United squad for the home league game against Leek CSOB.

Scored on his debut away to Chadderton FC on 19/4/2006.

Ormes, Gareth (Left back): Born 3/2/1983 in Pretoria, South Africa.

Gareth began playing football in the schools of Pretoria from a very early age.

As a 16-year-old he was selected to represent Pretoria – similar to our county system and a great honour, as only the best players from each club are chosen.

It was only when the first-choice left back broke his leg and Gareth stepped into the position that he really took to the role; otherwise he might not have had such great success on the field. He eventually joined Rentmeester Rangers in Immesdale, a club renowned for finding stars and who had just begun to operate a scheme with Manchester City whereby the player of the season was sent to Maine Road to train.

Rentmeester Rangers paid for Gareth to come to England after he was selected to train at Manchester City, but an overlap in the season meant that he couldn't join Manchester City. However, a scout from Maine Road recommended that non-league side Ramsbottom United trial him instead. Unfortunately, he didn't play enough games and he decided to move on, joining Prestwich Heys the following season. Although he stayed there for just over a season (2001/2), benefiting from regular football, including being on the losing side in the Goldline Trophy semi-final, he soon moved on and signed for rivals East Manchester FC and then Droylsden for the 2003/4 season. Meanwhile, he had a trial at Morecambe in 2003 which came to nothing.

Things didn't work out for him at Droylsden and after the opening 5 games he moved on again and re-joined East Manchester, where he finished the season.

Still searching for the right club, he moved to Salford City where, as luck would have it, he met player/coach Darren Lyons, who recognised his commitment and, when the season finished, Darren called Gareth to explain about the new club being formed and suggesting he try out. At Salford he teamed up with Barrie George and even replaced him in goal when Barrie was recalled to Radcliffe Borough.

Gareth attended the trials not knowing what to expect but, impressed by the turn out of trialists and the professionalism of the staff, he dug deep to make an impression.

All his efforts paid off and he made the squad and was selected for the first game against Leigh RMI.

Unfortunately, Gareth was struck down by a double hernia which laid him up for some time and he struggled to regain his form and fitness and he re-joined Ramsbottom United AFC in December 2006.

Orr, Adie (Forward): Born 22/2/1984 in Manchester.

Has the honour of scoring FC United's first cup goal against Cheadle Town in October. Orr then went on to score the club's first hat-trick in the 5-1 win. This gifted and very talented striker began as a trainee at Manchester City, where he played for the U19s in October 2001, and scored in the 7-1 win over Gillingham in the FA Youth Cup in January 2002. Adie joined Leigh RMI, transferring in the 2004 season, and then had a spell with Altrincham's reserves, making 10 appearances and scoring 6 goals, leaving in the summer of 2005. Adie was in the original squad and has been known to change the colour of his hair!

Ovechkin, Ilya:

Reserve Squad.

Ilya played in the pre-season friendly against Kirkham and Wesham in July 2006, unfortunately losing 1-0, but he scored in the opening game of the season in the 7-0 win over Padiham in August 2006.

Overseas Player: In their first season and despite being a non-league side, FC United boasts having overseas players in Gareth Ormes, who was born in Pretoria, South Africa, and Phil Power, who is Maltese.

Own Goals: Liam Foster scored on his debut in the 2006/7 season.

P

PA: The PA system is a professionally-run operation. The guys turn up early to make sure that the equipment works and prepare for the show. Peanut, Bobby and their assistant Simon lead the crowd in songs and making the necessary announcements.

Padiham: Padiham FC were formed in 1878, the same year as Manchester United, and it almost seems fitting that FC United's first home game is against them. The 'Caldersiders', as they were first known, were amongst the first football pioneers and were in at the start of the Lancashire Football Association and the LFA Senior Cup. Situated on the banks of the River Calder, hence the name 'Caldersiders', they fought for professionalism in football. The club's first ten years were a success, but when the Football League was established and money came into the game, Padiham found themselves unable to compete with their bigger neighbours and, as a result, gates fell and income was reduced. This left Padiham with little choice but to play in the minor local leagues or the Lancashire Combination League. At the end of the 1915/16 season, Padiham were finished. The war had taken the ground and the club was gone. It wasn't until after the Second World War that Padiham was reborn. 1,777 people turned out to see Padiham play their first game in the Lancashire Combination League at the Arbories Memorial Sports Ground in the clubs first game of the 1949/50 season The club fared well and became a founding member of the North West Counties Football League in 1982. They left the league in 1990, but returned after upgrading the Arbories Memorial Ground in 2001/2. Padiham have won many honours during their time, including the 'Burnley, Pendle and Rossendale Hospital Cup' twice in 1996 and 2005, Division Two winners 1971/72, Division Three winners 1983/84 and West Lancashire Football League winners in 1999/2000.

Paternity Leave: Simon Carden enjoyed paternity leave after the birth of his son during September.

Patterson, Rory (Forward): Born 16/7/1984 in Derry.

This fiery and talented striker began playing football from an early age and as a 10-year-old joined the local club, Moorfield

Celtic in Derry. He was at a club that went on foreign tours and the bond between the players was such that they won many overseas competitions and that drew attention from scouts from English clubs, many of whom came to see the phenomenon that is Rory Patterson. All the players knew that many of the talented 14- and 15-year-olds at Moorfield had been sent for trials at English clubs. Rory was excited to be going for a trial at Peterborough aged just 11.

Throughout his teenage years he had trials with Everton, Newcastle, Charlton and even his beloved Celtic!

It was eventually Rochdale that offered him a trial and they were so impressed by his determination and grit that they offered him a 3-year deal. The fans got their first treat of his potential when he came on as a second half substitute in a friendly against Accrington Stanley at the beginning of the 2001/2 season and again when he debuted against Bury in a LDV game, again as a sub. He made his league debut in an away game at Oxford, appearing as a sub. Over the seasons at the Dale he made most of his starts from the subs bench, but was unable to repeat his goalscoring touch seen in the reserves.

As a 19-year-old he was called up into the Eire U19 squad for the European Championship qualifiers, although he wasn't called upon to play.

During his time at Spotlands he was part of the famous cup team that took the club to the fifth round of the FA Cup with victories over Preston North End and Coventry before falling to Wolves.

During his spell at the Dale he played against noted opposition such as Manchester City with players of the calibre of David Seaman, Shaun Wright-Phillips and Robbie Fowler.

Alas, not all was well at the club and as Rory neared the end of his contract he fell victim to an injury and the club declined to renew the contract. Rory was surprisingly released by Rochdale at the end of the 2004/5 season. The supporters' 'Young Player of the Year' made 20 appearances during his 3 years of service.

Rory dropped to semi-professional football, joining Radcliffe Borough after a trial in July 2004 and signing a 2-year deal with the club. Even his short spell at Radcliffe Borough was eventful. His name appeared in a side that boasted Paul Gascoigne and former England captain Bryan Robson against a Manchester United XI. He played and scored in the side that beat current landlords Bury 4-1 and was included in the squad for the FA Cup game against Hereford United in the October. Rory found it difficult to combine work and football and left the club by mutual agreement in the November.

Shortly afterwards, he joined Mossley, appearing in a tight encounter against Chorley in the UniBond League Cup. During the period at Mossley he made 23 appearances, scoring the one goal, before leaving in June 2005.

Joining FC United began with a phone call from old friend Karl Marginson, who invited him to a 'behind closed doors' friendly against Woodley Sports and then in a more open game versus Stalybridge Celtic. It was at this game that the fans took Rory to their heart, nicknaming him 'Mr Mystery' or 'Man with no name' after wearing a shirt without a number on the back.

Rory's talents have given him a number of firsts: he scored the club's first goal in a home league game against Padiham; and became the first ever 'Man of the Month' for August 2005. That first goal against Padiham was also a first in so much as it was a penalty. Alas, he also has the dubious honour of being the first FCUoM player to be sent off in a cup game in the 2-1 defeat away to Colne. He did, however, score the winner in a very tight game against Winsford and then disappeared into the crowd to share his delight! Rory was voted the 'Player of the Year 2005/6' by the Non-League Paper.

Rory unfortunately missed the first penalty awarded to FC United in the FA Vase competition away to Padiham on 7th October 2006.

He was awarded the NWCFL 'Player of the Month' for March 2007, scoring 7 goals in the process.

In the last two home games of the 2006/7 season, Rory scored consecutive hat-tricks against Trafford and Formby.

Rory's 2006/7 season didn't end there, as he was awarded the Players' 'Player of the Season' and was also presented with the Russell Delaney Trophy, becoming the club's most decorated player.

To cap off Rory's season, he was voted the Non-League Paper's 'Young Player of the Year', with fans voting by e-mail overload for Rory to collect the award for the second year running.

Football Club United of Manchester

Created from despair - Powered by passion

Rory Patterson

Penalties:

First: FC United were awarded their first penalty in the home game against Padiham. The ever industrious Patterson was fouled, picked himself up and duly converted the penalty himself.

FC United's first penalty in a cup final was taken and scored by Nicky Platt in the 2006/7 season, helping to beat Curzon Ashton 2-1.

Saved: The first saved penalty goes to Steve Torpey. Playing at home against Norton United, he was upended in the penalty area and took the penalty himself. His effort was dispatched with aplomb, but the referee insisted upon its retake, having spotted an encroachment by a red shirt. The retake was saved.

Most: The most penalties awarded to FC United during the same game is 2 during the home defeat to Norton United, who themselves were awarded a penalty.

Phoenix, Jamie (Striker): Born 15/1/1984 in Crewe.

Jamie's talents began to show as early as seven, when his football skills were seen by the PE teacher and he was selected for the school team. His enthusiasm at playing centre forward paid off as his goalscoring prowess came to the notice of football league scouts and he was invited for a trial at Manchester City. The manager was the late great Alan Ball, who was so impressed by Jamie's goalscoring ability that the 9-year-old Phoenix was offered schoolboy terms.

Jamie progressed and early in the 1996/7 season he signed a 5-year contract, 3 years on a Youth Training Scheme (YTS) and 2 years on a professional contract. Alas, the management changed and it was time for Jamie to move on; but unfortunately Manchester City were reluctant to let him go and placed a high price tag on his contract, which other clubs were unable to agree with.

This goes to show how highly rated he was.

Jamie played Sunday league football until Bolton Wanderers decided to give him a trial aged 16. Jamie played in the FA Youth Cup against Port Vale and did well in the 1-0 win.

This move didn't work out for Jamie as homesickness took its toll and he returned home, but Jamie's talents hadn't gone unnoticed and he was offered a trial with Ipswich Town. Again for personal reasons, Jamie turned down Ipswich's offer, but Jamie's enthusiasm for the game found him at Sheffield Wednesday and he fought his way back to fitness and was promoted to the first team when he was struck down by injury.

Phoenix called it a day and 'fell out of love with the game'. He spent the next year chilling out with his mates, but he was determined not to quit football and a year later he signed for Nantwich Town after a brief spell at Altrincham.

He joined Altrincham late September 2002 and he came on as a substitute, making his full debut the following game. Unfortunately, he was sent off for a second yellow card and was immediately released. Jamie joined Nantwich Town in November 2003, leaving in March 2004 and joining Stafford Rangers in April

2004, debuting in the last game of the season against Dover Athletic.

This talented striker left Stafford Rangers after two full seasons in July 2006 and was welcomed at FC United, even though he almost signed for Walsall in February 2006. It was reported in a national newspaper that Jamie was late for a game after the motorway he was travelling on was closed due to an accident and that he ran 6½ miles along the hard shoulder. Unfortunately, he was too late to be named sub.

Made his league debut on 30th August 2006 in the 4-0 win over Flixton FC, where he came on as a substitute replacing Rory Patterson. His first senior goal came in the 3-0 win over Congleton Town in September 2006, when he again came on as a substitute. Jamie made his first start for the club in the record home league win 8-0 over Glossop North End in October 2006 and scored.

Made his FA Vase debut against Padiham, when he came on as a sub in October 2006.

Previous clubs: Manchester City, Sheffield Wednesday, Ipswich Town, Bolton Wanderers, Altrincham, Nantwich Town (3/4), Stafford Rangers.

Football Club United of Manchester

Created from despair - Powered by passion

Jamie Phoenix

Platt, Nick (Midfielder): Born 5/12/1087 in Ashton-under-Lyne.

A talented midfielder who couldn't wait to play football, having caught the bug as a 6-year-old but finding that he was too young to play for the U9s. But, having played in a 6-a-side tournament for Charlton Juniors, scouts from both Manchester United and Liverpool were so impressed that both clubs offered him a trial and then a placement. Nick accepted Liverpool's offer because the facilities for 9-year-olds was better, signing forms on 12th May 1996.

He stayed for 8 years and became a useful versatile utility player, which benefited both the coaches and the teams, teams he often went on to captain.

Unfortunately for him, being a utility player went against him and he was released, so alerting Burnley. He impressed Burnley and was offered a two-year apprenticeship playing for the U19s. He was made team captain in his second season and Burnley Youth went on to have their best cup run since the 1960s when they lost to Liverpool.

Despite the side doing so well, his contract wasn't renewed.

Trials with Carlisle and Accrington Stanley proved fruitless and he was advised to play non-league football, where his progress could be monitored.

He joined Stalybridge Celtic, but became disillusioned with their style of football. So he sent his CV to FC United manager Karl Marginson, who invited him down for a trial and he immediately felt at home.

Made his first appearance for FC United as a substitute against St Helen's Town in October 2006. On 28th October he made his first start for the club and scored in the record 8-0 win over Glossop North End. He also started in the Football League Challenge Cup game against Nantwich Town.

Nicky scored FC United's first penalty in a cup final, scoring from the spot to help FC United beat Curzon Ashton.

Previous clubs: Liverpool academy, Burnley youth.

Player of the Month: The first 'Player of the Month' award went to Rory Patterson for August. The award was sponsored by Under the Boardwalk.

Player of the Season: Naturally, all clubs have a player of the season who is voted for by the fans. Voting on the website and by fans at games was chosen as the means to elect the player most valued by the fans. The trophy was called 'The Russell Delaney Trophy' after Russell Delaney, a Board member who sadly passed away. Rory Patterson won the first award.

Rory Patterson also won the award for the 2006/7 season.

Players' Player of the Season: Karl Marginson presented Steven Spencer with the first ever presentation of the award after the last home game against Great Harwood Town.

Rory Patterson collected the honour for his performances during the 2006/7 season.

Manager's Player of the Season: A new award allowing the manager to reward his player of the season. The prize was earned by Rob Nugent for his sterling feats and goals during the 2006/7 season.

Reserves Players' Player of the Season: The reserves had an outstanding opening season, winning both the league and the cup. The player chosen by his team mates as exceptional was Adam Turner.

Manager's Reserves Player of the Season: Adam Turner was again selected by the manager as being the star amongst many stars and collected an amazing double award of his own.

U18s Players' Player of the Season: The foundation season was a great base for these players, who performed magnificently in their league. The player rated most highly by his team mates was Tony Tompos, who collected the team's first ever award.

Manager's U18s Player of the Season: Jamie Rother proved his worth to the side by being decorated by his manager.

Junior Supporters' Player of the Season: Joshua Howard won this award, presented by the junior supporters. He was presented with the trophy after the last home game of the season.

Pledges: By 8th July 2005, over 4,000 people had pledged money to FC United and the club had over £100,000 in the bank.

Postponed Games: The League Challenge Cup game away to Cheadle Town due to be played on 15th October 2005 wasn't signed off by the safety officials and the league decided that a change of venue and date were required. Discussions began between the two clubs and alternative venues proposed. The game was finally re-scheduled for Monday 17th October 2005 at Curzon Ashton's Tameside Stadium. The new venue has a ground capacity of 4,500, but the game had a restriction of 2,200 all-ticket.

The home game to Chadderton was postponed four times. It was postponed on 2nd November due to a waterlogged pitch, again on 30th November due to a frozen pitch and another waterlogged pitch prevented the tie being played on 15th February. The last postponement on 4th March 2006 was due to another frozen pitch.

League Games: The first league game to be postponed was the home game against Chadderton FC, the Gigg Lane pitch being waterlogged and the match called off after a pitch inspection. The re-scheduled Chadderton game was postponed for a second time as the pitch was frozen and re arranged for 15th February 2006 at 7.45pm.

Power, Phil (Assistant player/manager): Born 25/7/1966 in Malta.

Phil began his playing career with Northwich Victoria in the early 1980s and played in an FA Trophy final at Wembley when he was just 17. He then signed professional forms with Crewe Alexandria. This lasted 2 years before moving to Horwich (who are now Leigh RMI). Aged 20, he joined top Maltese side Sliema Wanderers, but came home – homesick. He joined Chorley, where he impressed Bournemouth's manager Harry Redknapp, but his move to Bournemouth collapsed when he suffered a double compound fracture in his leg during his farewell game. He spent two years recovering before spells with Barrow and Stalybridge and then moving on to join Sammy McIlroy at

Macclesfield Town. His honours include 2 England semi-professional caps, an FA Trophy, and he won 2 Vauxhall Conference titles. He left after 5 years to join Altrincham in 2001, becoming their player/coach; but he blotted his copybook by getting sent off twice. Phil made 76 appearances and scored 18 goals for Alty before signing for Radcliffe Borough and scoring on his debut. But he unfortunately missed the remainder of the season after being injured in a road traffic accident. Phil is also an ex-captain of England's amateur side. Phil had a spell at Bacup Borough before joining FCUoM. Phil made his FCUoM debut in the away visit to Ashton Town, coming on as a substitute for Joz Mitten. It was an eventful debut, as he had a goal disallowed on 81 minutes and collected a yellow card. Phil did open his account, scoring in the Division Two cup game against New Mills. FC United won 5-0. Phil works in the community as a social worker.

Priestley, Phil (Goalkeeper): Born 30/3/1979 in Wigan.

Phil was one of the first players to sign for FCUoM but was unfortunate to be injured for the pre-season friendlies and struggled to win back the goalkeeper's jersey from the impressive Barrie George. An experienced goalkeeper who has previously played in the UEFA Cup with Bangor City FC, he has also been on the books of Stalybridge Celtic, Prescot Cables, Rochdale, including loan spells at Scarborough and Chester City. He left the club amicably in September 2005 in order to play first-team football and joined Radcliffe Borough, having appeared in one league match for FC United.

Football Club United of Manchester
Created from despair - Powered by passion

Pritchard, Tony: Acting chairman until such time as one is elected.

Programmes: Programmes are part and parcel of the match-day routine and FC United are no exception. Some programmes were made available for the pre-season friendlies and league and cup programmes were produced as the norm. Programmes for friendlies became more desirable mid-season when FC United had a few weeks off due to bad weather, frozen pitches and fixture congestion. A hasty friendly was arranged against Woodley Sports. The short notice made it difficult for the printers and only 150 programmes were produced. These programmes were snapped up by the 800 or so eager fans who turned up to watch the game. The programmes sold for £1 were later sold on the auction site E-bay for £30-plus. Reprints were later available for £1.50. FC United won the game 4-2.

Promotion: To cap their first season in non-league football, FC United went on to win their division at the first attempt and collected the £400 winners' fee.

FC United gained promotion from the NWCFL Division 1 also at the first time of asking and joined the re-structured pyramid in the UniBond Northern League, gaining back-to-back promotions.

Pyramid: The Football Pyramid is the name given to semi-professional clubs below the main Football League. The official name is 'The National League System'. FC United is at step 10 – that is 9 steps below the Premiership.

The system follows:

1. Premiership
2. Championship
3. League One
4. League Two
5. Nationwide Conference
6. Conference North/South
7. UniBond Premier
8. UniBond One
9. North West Counties Division One
10. North West Counties Division Two (FC United).

Non-league football begins at the Nationwide Conference. Two clubs are promoted to League Two and two are relegated. Promotion to the Nationwide Conference comes from two divisions, the Conference North and South. Promotion to the Conference North and South comes from three divisions from three leagues: the UniBond League, the Ryman League and the Southern League. The champions are promoted along with the winners of play-offs in each division, making 6 teams in total. When all the teams are known, they are then allocated North or South. The play-off involves teams placed 2nd to 5th in each league. The UniBond and Ryman Leagues have a feeder division, whist the Southern League has two: Southern League East and Southern League Midlands & West. Below the 'Pyramid' there is a huge spread of regional and local clubs. The feeders into the UniBond League are from the North West Counties Division One, the Northern Counties East Premier Division and the Albany Northern League Division One. This is generalised, as clubs who gain promotion are based on location, but some clubs also fit

Football Club United of Manchester
Created from despair - Powered by passion

equally into differing divisions based on location. Only one team is promoted from and relegated to the North West Counties Division One, whereas there are two teams promoted into the North West Counties Division One from the NWCFL Division Two (FC United).

At the end of the 2005/6 season, the Football Association are implementing a restructuring of the 'Pyramid' which currently incorporates the UniBond 1st Division. The FA plans to extend the current four divisions to five so that the Isthmian League splits into two divisions, replicating the Southern League. This means that more teams will be needed to play at this level to fill the spaces. The UniBond League are pressurising the FA to allocate them an extra division in line with the Isthmian and Southern Leagues. If granted, more teams will be promoted, meaning that, provided FC United get promoted, a number of teams in Division One will already have moved on!

During the summer the FA allowed the structuring of the pyramid and FC United became a Step 5 team and during the 2006/7 season a further re-structuring saw FC United apply for level 4 status and the UniBond League.

Q

Quarter-Final: FC United's first quarter-final was in the Division Two Trophy against Nelson FC at home on 4th February 2006. FC United had been handed a bye in round one and beaten New Mills 5-0 in the second round.

R

Radio: During FC United's second season, Mike Box commentated live from the Willows for FC United's game against Salford City in the 2nd round of the FA Vase on 18th November 2006.

Dave Chadwick, FC United's injured captain, was a second half guest on the radio during the Atherton Collieries game on Wednesday 29th November 2006.

'Swampy', aka Steve Bennett, and Bryan Hancock provide radio commentary for the fans' radio station.

Radio Interviews: Andy Walsh was interviewed for the BBC Radio 4 programme on 13th December 2005 to discuss his decision to give up his season ticket to Old Trafford. A fan was invited onto the BBC's 5 Live talk show to talk about going to Gigg Lane and watch FC United play.

Randles, Greg:

Greg attended trials in June and was invited to the pre-season friendlies. He came on as a sub in the 5-2 victory over Flixton, scoring the fifth goal. He left shortly afterwards.

Rawlinson, Mark (Midfielder): Born 9/6/1975 in Bolton.

Mark had football in his blood and was keen to get involved, finally getting into Mossbank Juniors as an 11-year-old. His commitment and love of the game saw him selected to play for the school team and from there Bolton Town came calling. Aged 14, the youth scout from Manchester United spotted Mark's gift and invited him to Old Trafford.

Mark would go anywhere to see or play a game of football and was playing at Everton, Bolton and Manchester United when he had to make a choice and, naturally being a huge Red fan, he chose Manchester United. When he left school at 16 he was offered an apprenticeship at Old Trafford and became one of 'Fergie's Fledglings', along with David Beckham, Ben Thornley and his close friend Gary Neville.

He trained at Manchester United during the years 1993–5, a year behind David Beckham, a youth side full of confidence having won the Youth FA Cup and replacing the older members of the first team. Alas, Mark didn't quite make it with his friends and AFC Bournemouth showed an interest in him.

Opting to move and get regular football, Mark then spent 5 years at AFC Bournemouth, scoring twice in 79 appearances before joining Exeter City in 2000. He had a brief spell at Weymouth, where he was their penalty taker, and made 25 appearances, scoring 3 times, before being released and then joining Dorchester Town FC on a free transfer. He then had a trial with Altrincham in July 2004 prior to signing for FCUoM.

Mark retired from football due to injury.

Red Cards:

First: Rory Patterson was the first FCUoM player to be sent off. Unusually, though, from the bench! It happened in the 2-1 cup defeat to Colne. He had already been substituted and was sitting on the subs bench when a scuffle broke out nearby and Patterson was judged by the referee to have thrown a punch and was duly red carded. Joz Mitten was the first player to be sent off whilst still on the park against Castleton Gabriels in December 2005 when he became involved in a minor altercation with a Castleton player on 86 minutes. James Gilbert, the Castleton Gabriels player, was also sent off and so became the first player to be sent off against FC United.

Joz Mitten appealed against the red card but was found guilty and given a 7-day suspension beginning on Monday 13th February and a £10 fine.

Most: The most FC United players sent off in a game is two. Again in a cup game, the FA Vase. It happened during the home tie to Quorn FC on 9th December 2006, when Liam Coyne was given a straight red card for pushing a Quorn player who went down like a lead balloon! Josh Howard was sent off for two yellow cards.

During the 2006/7 season, FC United players were shown a total of 6 red cards: 3 league and 3 cup.

Referee:

League: Rob Goodwin-Davey from Handforth has the honour of being the first referee to officiate a league match between Leek CSOB and FC United. Mr Gerry Wild and Dave Chritchlow were the assistant referees. The referee for the first home game was Ryan Bromfield, whose assistants were Keith Greenhalgh and Peter Adamson for the Padiham game.

Football Club United of Manchester
Created from despair - Powered by passion

League Challenge Cup: In the first League Challenge Cup game between Cheadle Town FC and FC United, played in October 2005, the referee was B Lamb, with assistants G Barker and A Tomlinson.

League Challenge Cup Final: The honour of presiding over FC United's first cup final went to referee Paul Tierney; his assistants were Peter Gooch and Alex Gear. The fourth official was Dean Mohareb.

Division Two Cup: Mr P B Birch was the referee in the Division Two Cup game against Colne, with P Adamson and A Tomlinson assisting.

Reserve Division Cup Final: Mr Mike Conroy has the privilege of being the first referee to officiate in a cup final for FC United reserves.

Renee, Mike (Defender).
Reserve Squad.

Reserve Team: As FC United progressed through their first season it became apparent that another source of players would be needed. A small squad depleted by injury, suspensions and holidays highlighted the need to rotate players. As much as the players enjoyed playing, wanted to play and in many cases were playing, training as well as working week in and week out, it revealed the need for a larger squad.

The plans for the youth and reserve teams were part of the initial blueprint of the club. Regardless of the success of the senior team, both the reserve and youth teams would provide many local talented youngsters with the opportunity of staying in football, nurturing their skills and being selected to play at a higher level through the first team.

Both youth and reserve teams will be introduced in the 2006/7 season.

Tony Cullen was selected to be the club's first reserve team manager, having played for the club. Tony is assisted by Lawrence Greenhalgh.

The reserve team played in the North West Counties Reserve League (NWCRL).

Having opened their account with a resounding 7-0 victory, the reserve side went on to claim the title with three games to spare, scoring 157 goals, conceding 36, and winning 36 of the 42 games, drawing 4 and only losing 2 – such was their combined talent.

The reserves were accepted into the Mid Cheshire League Division Two for the 2007/8 season.

Reserve Team Players:

Dale Newbrook (Goalkeeper): Born 18/10/82

Warren Collier (Defender): Born 13/10/86

Ben Mortimer (Defender): Born 4/6/85

Liam Foster (Defender): Born 4/9/1987 in Salford

Shaun Roscoe (Defender): Born 15/8/1986

Michael Sack (Defender): Born 6/7/87

Ryan Stewart (Defender): Born 28/3/87

Football Club United of Manchester

Created from despair - Powered by passion

Anthony O'Neil (Defender)

Adam Turner (Defender): Born 31/12/86

Martin Cosgrave (Midfielder)

Kyle Harrop (Midfielder): Born 22/4/87

Ilya Ovechkin (Midfielder): Born 23/11/85

Ryan Shaughnessy (Midfielder): Born 19/2/88

Fernando Vaz Te (Midfielder): Born 8/7/85

Danny Allen (Forward)

Gary Edwards (Forward): Born 10/8/86

Louie Scott (Forward): Born 5/3/88

Danny Shannon (Forward)

Sam Robertson (Pos)

Ricardo Brandao

Renee Mike (Defender)

Matt Easter.

Stephen Varley.

Adam Green.

Lee Bushel.

Tavares Ellisio.

Robertson, Sam (Position): Born 11/10/1985 in Dundee.

Reserve Squad.

Sam played for FC United's reserve team against Abbey Hey and made an instant impression. Sam also played in the friendly game against Kirkham and Wesham, which they unfortunately lost. This star also played Adam Barlow in 'Coronation Street' and is no slouch when it comes to football.

Roscoe, Shaun (Defender): Born 15/8/1986 in Manchester.

Reserve Squad.

As a 6-year-old, Shaun Roscoe began making a name for himself playing for Droylsden Juniors in an Under-9 league. Shortly after, he moved to Heyside, where he played on the left wing and he grew quicker than the others. His height advantage frightened defenders and during one season he scored 93 goals, including 8 in one game.

His goalscoring achievements drew attention from the scouts and Rochdale offered the 13-year-old goal machine a chance to shine.

An unfortunate accident saw Roscoe play at left back, a position he took to like a duck to water, and the goal machine became a shot-stopper.

When he finished school he took his skills to Bury, who liked what they saw and offered the 16-year-old a 2-year YTS contract, which they extended a further year. The youth team coach, Chris Casper, took Roscoe under his wing and instilled in him the importance of being fit and disciplined, a trait that benefited both Roscoe and the youth side as they claimed the youth team title and won a cup knockout competition. This was also a time that saw Shaun captain the side on occasions.

Football Club United of Manchester
Created from despair - Powered by passion

After a constructive two-year period and opportunity to make his 1st team appearance, Shaun picked up a serious Achilles heel injury, an injury gained by working himself too hard. Roscoe came to a painful decision and that was to leave Bury, a move that Bury accepted with reluctance.

Three months later, a rejuvenated Roscoe took to the playing field, signing for Conference side Accrington Stanley. The first season went well for Shaun, but he came down with a dose of the mumps, which sidelined him again and he left Accrington Stanley.

During the summer, Chris Casper put Roscoe in touch with manager Karl Marginson and he was invited to join the reserve team with Tony Cullen.

Shaun soon showed what he was capable of and he impressed during his first season. Shaun made his first senior appearance in the FA Vase cup game against Quorn. Since then he has become a regular member of the first team.

He made his home debut on 30th December 2006 in the league game against Newcastle Town.

Rudd, Stuart (Striker): Born 10/10/1976 in Wigan.

"You'll never be a great goalscorer but you will be a scorer of great goals"; so said the great Ian Rush when commenting on Stuart Rudd. The same quality was seen by Wigan manager Paul Jewel when he scored against them in a pre-season game and he found out that Wigan had rejected him!

Stuart began his football career as a midfielder/right back; it wasn't until later that he changed position. That move came when he played for his school team and earned him a trial at Wigan Town, and he was selected. Now he became serious about his football and his dedication was rewarded by trials at Wigan Athletic and Bolton Wanderers. It was a difficult decision for a 13-year-old to make and although he chose Wigan he regretted Wigan not having the same training facilities.

He performed well for the youth side despite a lack of opportunity and investment, but he was part of a young youth side that thrashed Newcastle United and Manchester United youth teams, even though the Manchester United side contained mega-stars David Beckham, Paul Scholes, Ryan Giggs and the Neville brothers. But still it wasn't enough to earn him selection and his time at Wigan was over.

Stuart left school and became a damn fine bricklayer, helping to rebuild the home of Wigan Athletic. With injury and the lack of football, he endured an enforced break from the game.

He joined Daisy Hill as an 18-year-old, teaming up with future team mate Dave Chadwick and scoring some 30 goals in 20 games, and so impressed the Skelmersdale manager that he joined them for the 1998/9 season. He scored a mere 22 goals and was still upset at not scoring more when most seasoned professionals would give their eye-teeth to achieve that number.

It was whilst at Skelmersdale that the pre-season friendly against Wigan occurred and the story goes that Paul Jewel was angry that the teenage prodigy who had scored a brace against them was in fact rejected by them.

The following season he hit the net 24 times in 54 games,

helping Skelmersdale to the NWCFL Cup and the 4th round of the FA Cup.

Burscough were immediately alerted and paid a record £2,500 to Skelmersdale for his services, but his time at Burscough didn't work out and he returned to Skelmersdale, regaining his Midas touch and scoring 28 goals in 24 outings. He was made team captain for the 2001/2 season and he led from the front, scoring 46 times in 43 appearances in the 2002/3 season – a feat matched in the following season, except it only took him 38 games to reach that total. He won the League's Golden Boot and was rewarded with a 3-year contract.

Skelmersdale United were promoted to the UniBond in 2005/6 and there was a management change, an unnecessary change in the views of some, and a number of players including Stuart left the club. He had scored an amazing 229 goals in 308 games, breaking Tommy Tinsley's record of 215 goals, which had stood since 1948.

He joined FC United and made his home debut against AFC Wimbledon.

Stuart was the first FC player to have a goal disallowed in the FA Vase cup competition when his second half effort against Brodsworth MW was cancelled out for offside. FC United went on to win 3-1 with Stuart, a pre-season signing, scoring FC United's first campaign goal.

However, this didn't stop him from continuing his scoring and he finished the 2006/7 season as the club's top scorer with 45 goals.

Stuart Rudd

Russell Delaney Supporters' Player of the Season Award: An award presented in honour of Russell Delaney, who sadly passed away during the struggle to get FC United founded. The player voted for by the fans at games and on-line was Rory Patterson, who collected the award from Mrs Delaney after the home game against Great Harwood Town.

Rory Patterson also won the award for the second year in a row for his outstanding performances during the 2006/7 season.

S

Sacks, Michael (Defender): Born 6/7/1987.
Reserve Squad.

Michael attended the trials held in June and was in the historic side that played in the first ever game for the reserves. The friendly played against Flint Town United was won 1-0 in front of 900 travelling fans. He was outstanding, according to manager Tony Cullen. Mike played in the friendly that was lost to Kirkham and Wesham in July 2006.

Mike has captained the side on occasions and plays regularly for the reserves.

He scored in the opening 7-0 win over Padiham in August 2006.

Mike was named in the victorious cup final squad that beat Padiham 4-1, though not used.

Sampson, Gary (Midfielder): Born 13/9/1982 in Manchester.

As a lad he played football for the famous Stretford Vics football club. The standard of football amongst these youngsters was of such a high pedigree that scouts from both Manchester City and United were frequently at the games. Playing with no fear, he impressed the visiting Manchester United so much that he was asked to go to Manchester United's School of Excellence at The Cliff. He advanced to U17s and U19s. A tough midfielder, he made it as far as United's second XI. His reserve team debut came in a game against Liverpool. Unfortunately, his time in the reserves was limited to playing mainly in the U19s. He signed apprentice forms on 5/7/99, turning professional on 12/7/2000. In the 2001/2 season he made 27 U17 appearances, scoring once, made 2 reserve appearances, and turned out twenty times for the U19s, scoring twice, and made 3 youth cup appearances.

Sir Alex had no doubts about his talent, remarking that he wouldn't have stayed so long at Old Trafford if he didn't have talent; but he was released by Manchester United FC in the summer of 2002. Brief try-outs with Bury and Macclesfield didn't work out and Gary joined UniBond outfit Accrington Stanley. Despite his time there, he never quite made the first team and he joined Radcliffe Borough on 13/12/2003 and left on 20/2/6 to join the Royal Marines. After training with the marines, it became time to either sign up or walk away. Fortunately for FC United, the talents of Gary had been seen at Radcliffe Borough by Karl Marginson and he was asked to join FC United.

He came on as a sub in the cup game against Nantwich town on 11th November 2006 and made his league debut against Stone Dominoes in the same month.

Unfortunately for FC United, Gary suffered an injury that kept him out of football for the latter part of the season and he left the club, re-signing for Radcliffe Borough prior to the 2007/8 season.

Score Draws:

League: There were 5 score draws in the inaugural season, all 1-1, except one which ended 3-3.

There were only 4 score draws in the second season, again all ending 1-1 except one, which ended 4-4.

Score Draws Cup: There was one score draw in the League Challenge Cup semi-final 1st leg against old foe Congleton Town: 2-2 in March 2007.

Football Club United of Manchester
Created from despair - Powered by passion

Scott, Louie (Forward): Born 5/3/1988.

Reserve Squad.

Louie played in the pre-season friendlies and scored in the 3-2 loss to Warrington Town in August 2006. He played in the opening game of the season, scoring the reserves' first hat-trick in the 7-0 win over Padiham in August 2006.

Semi-Final: FC United's first opponents in a cup semi-final were Congleton Town. The semi-final was in the D-Zine (Contractors) Ltd Challenge Cup in March 2007. The ties were played over 2 legs: away on 15th March and home on 31st March. The first game ended in a 2-2 draw, with Rhodri Giggs having the honour of scoring FC United's first semi-final goal. FC United won the second leg 4-3, twice coming from behind and despite being a man down. Stuart Rudd scored FC United's first and second goals.

Shannon, Danny (Forward).

Reserve Squad.

Danny made his first team debut in the 8-0 win over Squires Gate, getting his name on the score sheet after coming off the bench to head home number eight.

The game, played in front of 2,378 fans, saw FC United go 10 points clear at the top of Division 1.

Previously, Danny played for Woodley Sports Youth, scoring in the 5-1 thrashing of Morecambe Youth Academy B in the Alliance Open Cup.

He also played in an impressive 3-1 win at Toxteth Liverpool, scoring two brilliant goals and earning the 'Man of the Match' award.

Shaughnessy, Ryan (Midfielder).

Reserve Squad.

Ryan was making headlines as far back as the U13s when he scored a penalty in the top-of-the-table clash between Bury Juniors and Avro U13s. His penalty, scored after only 5 minutes, opened the floodgates and Avro won 5-0.

Ryan was in the squad to face Kirkham and Wesham in a friendly match in July 2006.

Simms, Chris (Midfielder): Born 10/10/1966 in Salford.

It was during his time at Woodhouse Park Juniors as a 16-year-old that he impressed the scouts from Stockport County and he was invited to attend weekly training sessions at Stockport College and was eventually given his break.

It was also here that he lost his confidence and he left Stockport County. A year later his confidence was restored with success at Maine Road FC.

Now aged 24, he joined UniBond side Hyde United, who were also enjoying huge success by reaching the FA Cup first round, the semi-final of the FA Trophy and retaining the Manchester Premier Cup.

A short spell in Lower Hutt, New Zealand, followed, where a 7-month contract became a 4-month contract when he came home unexpectedly. The manager of Maine Road FC stepped in and paid off the debt to Lower Hutt and Simms joined Maine Road for his second spell. Hitting a rich scoring vein, Chris was signed up by Trafford FC in the 1996/7 season and helped Trafford to the North West Counties League Championship, Manchester Senior Cup and North West Counties League Challenge Trophy finals. As he approached 30, he left Trafford and rejoined Maine Road and tried to help the club out of a difficult situation by becoming the player/manager in 2001/2. Unfortunately, the club was relegated. Maine Road continued with their new boss and Chris rang the changes by bringing in new faces and his faith was repaid when they finished 3rd in his first full season and the following year 2003/4 they earned promotion back to Division One and enjoyed a good FA Cup run, lining the coffers along the way.

A huge Manchester United fan, 'Simmo' appreciated what FC United were trying to do and wanted to do his bit to help, even if it meant dropping a division and giving up the player/manager status he had enjoyed with successful Maine Road FC. Chris made over 512 appearances for Maine Road, scoring nearly 130 goals over a four-year period before leaving Maine Road in December 2005 to join FC United. He was on the subs bench for the 1-1 away draw to Flixton FC. The ex-Hyde United man had earlier sustained a groin injury making a guest appearance for FC United in a pre-season friendly.

He made his first start against Nelson on 15th January 2006 to fill the gap left by the injured Simon Carden. He scored his first goal in the home game against Holker Old Boys on 25th February 2006.

In June 2006 Chris retired from the first team to manage FC United's Under 18s.

Smallest Player: The smallest player in the 2005/6 season was reputed to be Will Ahern.

Smith, Steve (Midfielder): Born 9/6/1984 in Salford.

Football life began as a striker with all the glamour that it attracts, but for this mega-talented lad it was in the midfield that he really felt at home, getting stuck into the action.

As an 8-year-old experiencing competitive football at school, Steve was excited enough to join a club and joined Deane, along with a number of his school mates. Despite this team spirit, Steve craved a bigger challenge and joined nearby Boothstown Boys Club. The standard wasn't as high, but Steve still earned the coach's praise as a prolific striker; but in spite of this he moved to the midfield to emulate his older brother.

It was on a football trip to Germany that he really shone and a scout from Manchester invited him for a trial at League Two club Rochdale. Fellow FC United team mate Rory Patterson was already at Rochdale and on hand to offer words of advice and Steve survived the elimination rounds, earning himself a 3-year scholarship: a big deal for a 16-year-old teenager and which cemented his decision to become a professional footballer.

Smith began brightly in the first year, breaking into the first team; but the youth team manager left and Steve was unable to maintain the same relationship with the next two managers and in the third year Smith knew he wasn't going to be offered a contract and he left.

Bury was Steve's next port of call and after a two-month trial he left, frustrated because he was equal to the talent of the squad

Football Club United of Manchester
Created from despair - Powered by passion

but the manager needed better players to fit in with the limited budget he had available.

However, he gained valuable experience which he took down the road to Leigh RMI, where he stayed for the next two years, enjoying the camaraderie and playing on high-quality pitches up and down the country.

It was during a friendly against FC United, a team he hardly knew about, that he really felt the buzz of playing in front of large crowds.

Steve had a short spell with Conference North side Lancaster City towards the end of the 2005/6 season when he was given manager Karl Marginson's number. A phone call later and he has never looked back. His first appearance was from the subs bench in the first league game against St Helen's and his first start came against Trafford, when he scored the only goal of the game and soaked in the adulation of the screaming fans.

He was released in November 2006 and joined Leek Town.

Songs: Songs from the terraces, of which there are many, include such favourites as "Head shoulders knees and toes", "My old man's a dustman" and "Drunken Sailor". Naturally the words have been changed! One of the most popular being "We don't care about Rio, he don't care about me", in reference to his greed and not worrying about the fans. A band from Salford called Hanky Park teamed up with Peter Hook and released a single called "We'll never die" in protest at the takeover of Manchester United.

Spencer, Steve (Defender): Born 6/10/1981 in Wythenshawe.

Steve began his playing career at Sale United as an 8-year-old and it wasn't until he turned 14 that he joined the famous Stretford Vics football club. It was during his time at the Vics that he experienced European football, playing against esteemed sides such as PSV Eindhoven. It wasn't until he turned 16 that he decided to make football a career after a scout from Bolton saw him play and was that impressed he offered Steve schoolboy forms to sign. Unfortunately, he wasn't offered a Youth Training Scheme (YTS) place and he was released. Determined not to give up, he turned up for trials at Sheffield United a day later and earned a YTS place.

He had a productive first year and his hard work paid off, but the second year was better. He was made youth team captain, gained experience in the reserve side and even scored the winning goal against Blackburn Rovers at Ewood Park in a youth FA Cup game.

Towards the end of his term he was loaned out to Rochdale and eventually released by Sheffield United at the end of the season.

This second knock-back affected his confidence, but he soon came back, signing for Leigh RMI from October 2002 to the following May, only to find regular football hard to come by; so, after a few games, he moved on, this time joining Radcliffe Borough for the 2003/4 season and stayed. He was now playing regular football but an injury forced him to take a break. It was during the break that he caught up with an old friend from his Sheffield days, Rob Nugent, who informed him of FC United; but it wasn't until manager Karl Marginson saw him play that he was invited down to Gigg Lane.

Steve played in a friendly and was so amazed by the professionalism of the club, the enthusiasm of the players and the fans that he signed the following day.

Steve has the privilege of scoring FCUoM's first ever competitive away goal against Leek CSOB and followed that up with his and the club's second goal. He was voted the 'Players' Player of the Season' for the 2005/6 season.

Sponsorship:

Sponsorship Scheme: A sponsorship scheme called the '127 Club' allows small- to medium-sized businesses as well as individuals and bigger interests to sponsor the club. The draw was made at the Daisy Hill game and the main sponsor for the 2005/6 season would be the 'Bhopal Medical Appeal'. The name will appear on the club's website and on letterheads, but the Board made the decision not to have the sponsors' names on the shirts. Another vote next season may reverse this decision.

Sponsor: The Bhopal Medical Appeal supported FC United by taking out an advert in the club programme for the entire 2005/6 season and the FC United supporters group reciprocated by holding collections at games for the appeal fund. The Appeal Fund raised money in order to buy essential medical equipment to treat the residents of Bhopal. They suffered as a result of a deadly gas leak from The Union Carbide plant in their town. One of the members of FC United is a founder member and persuaded The Bhopal Appeal Fund to take out a regular advert, as they were both fighting corporate greed.

Players: A decision was made to allow individual sponsorship of the manager and players. For £200 plus VAT you could have your name, company name or logo underneath the image of your choice in the programme. Sponsorship lasts for a year.

Squad: The original squad of players listed on 14th July 2005 to face Leigh RMI was: Tony Coyne, Kevin Elvin, Craig Fleury, Barrie George, Ryan Gilligan, Matt Haley, Ryan Hevicon, Darren Lyons, Billy McCartney, Rob Nugent, Joz Mitten, Paul Mitten, Gareth Ormes, Adie Orr, Phil Power, Phil Priestley, Mark Rawlinson, Steve Torpey, Rob Trees and Matt Weston.

Steering Group: The Steering Group consists of 16 members designed to deal with the running of the club.

The 16 are: Luc Zentar, Andy Walsh, Vasco Wackrill, Jules Spencer, Phil Sheeran, Tony Pritchard, John-Paul O'Neill, Peter Munday, Martin Morris, Tony Jordan, Andrew Howse, Russell Delaney, Adam Brown, Robert Brady, Phil Bedford and Mike Adams. Sadly and with great sorrow Russell Delaney passed away on Tuesday 1st November 2005 after a long illness. Russell, using his vast knowledge and host of football contacts, was crucial in the fight to stop Murdoch and gave invaluable advice and assistance during the supporters' fight against Glazer. Russell played a vital and monumental role in the forming of FC United of Manchester. His diligence and good humour will be missed.

Football Club United of Manchester
Created from despair - Powered by passion

Stewart, Ryan (Defender): Born 28/3/87.

Reserve Squad.

Born in Salford, this 19-year-old Manchester United fan is fighting for his place after injury. Plays at left back and has been in and out of the side following injuries.

He featured heavily in defence for the reserves but is yet to break into the first team.

Previous clubs include: Rochdale, Trafford and Flixton. He joined Winsford United during the 2006/7 season.

Streaker: There were not one but three streakers at Hilton Park at FCUoM's away friendly against Leigh RMI.

Strip: The home strip is a red shirt, white shorts and black socks. The away strip is white shirts, black shorts and black socks. During the set-up of the club, the away strip hadn't been prepared. When the fixture against Leigh RMI came about, Leigh wanted to play in their new home strip of red and white with the new sponsors' logo. When it became apparent that FCUoM only had their home strip available and that clashed with Leigh's, Bill Taylor, Chairman of Leigh RMI, arranged to send their away strip – which still had the old sponsor on it – to their suppliers in Nottingham, a round trip of 160 miles, who replaced the logo and sent the strip back in double-quick time.

The fans voted on new home shirts during the 2006/7 season with FC United announcing a competition to design the strip.

Stopford, Mark: Director of Operations. Nicknamed 'Cheetham' for some unknown reason; runs a smooth ship controlling the volunteers, ball boys and the general running of the club.

Substitute:

League: The first ever FC United substitute was Darren Lyons. He replaced Craig Fleury at half time in the game away to Leek CSOB on 13th August 2005 in the first league game of the season.

Scott Holt was the first substitute to be used in a home game when he replaced Mark Rawlinson on 66 minutes against Padiham.

Cup: Chris Simms came on for Steve Torpey in the first half of extra time in the Division Two Cup game against Nelson in February, and the first substitute used in the League Challenge Cup was Mark Rawlinson, who came on for Steve Spencer in the game against Cheadle Town on 17th October 2005. Manager Karl Marginson tends to use all of his substitutes each game, but in a friendly game against Leigh RMI he utilised 10 substitutions with only goalkeeper Barrie George playing the full 90 minutes.

Supporters: As on the first day against Leek CSOB, when 2,590 fans turned out to see FC United play, a record for the North West Counties Football League (NWCFL), the number exceeded the combined attendance for Leek for the entire previous season. In doing so, this game became the first in English history for a non-league match where the visiting fans were escorted away from the ground by the police. Over 63,000 saw FC United play in the first six months.

Football Club United of Manchester
Created from despair - Powered by passion

Suspension: The first FCUoM player to serve a ban was new boy Joshua Lincoln Howard. Joshua had signed for the club in early November and made his debut on 15th November in the cup game away to Colne FC. Four days later he began the first of a 2-match ban for a red card he received whilst playing for Mossley back in April. Bizarrely, it was in the Colne game that the first FCUoM sending-off occurred. The player to be shown the red card was Rory Patterson and he was on the substitutes' bench at the time, having been replaced earlier. It happened in the dying moments with FC United trailing 2- 1. FC United won a throw and wanted to take it quickly, but Colne had other ideas and prevented it. A scuffle broke out and Rory joined in. His behaviour was deemed violent by the referee and the red card was brandished. He was the first player to receive a red card as a FC United player. His suspension was for 35 days from 9th January to 12th February, and a fine of £25.

Supporters Group: The address of the supporters group is:

FCUoM Supporters Group,
Suite 116,
111 Piccadilly,
Manchester,
M1 2HX.

The website URL is: **www.fcunitedofmanchester.co.uk**.

Membership is free and application can be made online.

There are branches in Bury, Central Manchester, Blackpool, Cheshire, Swindon, Midlands, Stockport, Shropshire, Warrington and Yorkshire. Branches also exist in Sweden, Spain, New Zealand, Wales, Warsaw, Scandinavia, Canada, and Holland.

During October 2005 the Supporters Group set up a Junior Supporters Group, with the ability to select their own club chairman, vice-chair and secretary. These under 16s would be able to discuss fundraising, day trips and the Christmas Party.

Swarbrick, Dave (Striker): Born 14/4/1984 in Barrow.

As a 4-year-old Dave began kicking the ball around with gusto and quickly joined his father's football team, Holker Old Boys. Sheffield Wednesday began trials around the local area and Dave was asked to go along, but he declined. A knee injury forced a year-long break, but Dave fought back to fitness and gained his place in the U18s and then the reserves.

Dave's hard work hadn't gone unnoticed and Barrow FC came in for the dedicated 17-year-old and he made his debut in a cup game against Accrington Stanley, where he scored in the 3-2 win, cementing a good performance.

Whilst he was playing for Barrow his former team mates were lining up to play against FC United and he went along to watch. Taken aback by the atmosphere and not having the best of times at Barrow led him to re-join Holker Old Boys and he found himself lining up against FC United. He scored in the loss, but his skill and desire came to Karl Marginson's attention. A week later Dave was persuaded to join FC United and he made his debut in a friendly against Woodley Sports and enjoyed European success playing in the friendly against Leipzig. His full debut came in the loss to Flixton, but he has never looked back. Unfortunately, his injured knee meant having surgery and missing most of the 2006/7 season.

Football Club United of Manchester
Created from despair - Powered by passion

T

Table:

The final league position for FC United's inaugural season:

Division Two									
Pos	Club	P	W	D	L	GF	GA	GD	Pts
1	FC United (C) (P)	36	27	6	3	111	35	76	87

The final league position for the 2006/7 season:

Division One									
Pos	Club	P	W	D	L	GF	GA	GD	Pts
1	FC United (C) (P)	42	36	4	2	157	36	121	112

C = Champions. P = Promoted.

Takeovers: During the summer of discontent and the idea of a new football club in Manchester was being mooted around, another plan came to light. Instead of forming a new club, why not take over an existing club? Leigh RMI were in difficulties and ripe for a takeover. It was decided that it had to be a new club because it would enable the fans to go back to enjoying football and to be able to hold it dear and say "That's ours!" The United fans, having been steam-rollered by Glazer in a hostile takeover, felt it would be unfair to impose such feelings upon the Leigh RMI fans, so the takeover was decided against and the idea was shelved. Both clubs have remained friends and pledged to help each other.

Tallest Player: The tallest player during the 2005/6 season was newcomer Matthew Higgins at 6'5". Keeper Higgins was signed midway through the season.

Tavares, Ellisio:

Reserve Squad.

Listed in the squad to face Kirkham and Wesham in a friendly match in July 2006.

Taylor, Matthew (Defender): Born 5/12/1980 in Cheshire.

Matty began his football career as a goalkeeper with Fletcher Moss Boys and had Wes Brown, the Manchester United player, as a defender. The team did well and Matty became bored with life in goal and spent more and more time running the ball out of goal. Matty's teacher put him forward for trials with Manchester Boys, a side created from the cream of the local schoolboys. Matty won himself a place. He played in tournaments up and down the country and even against Steven Gerrard at Liverpool. Eventually, he was picked to play for Greater Manchester Boys, which was an even bigger compliment; but he was unable to gain a YTS place with any professional club.

He left school at 16 and played football for Moss Amateurs and established himself as an attacking right back.

Mike McKenzie picked up on Matty's talent and he signed for Hyde United, a UniBond side a few divisions above Moss Amateurs.

Matty made his debut in the home game against Runcorn in

November 1998 and enjoyed the next three years, earning himself the players' 'Player of the Year' award in his second season and the supporters' 'Player of the Year' in his third.

He played his last game in November 2002, making 119 appearances and scoring 4 goals. Leaving Hyde was difficult, but he went in search of a new challenge and Mossley – who were considered the non-league version of Chelsea because of the money they had – made Matty an offer he couldn't refuse and in 2002 he joined Mossley and manager Ally Pickering.

It was also here at Mossley that he met Karl Marginson, Josh Howard, Leon Mike and Phil Melville and, despite a reasonably successful 3-year spell at Mossley, a change of manager meant a change of direction and he was released in May 2005.

Ally Pickering was now manager at Woodley Sports and in August 2005 Matty teamed up with Pickering at Woodley as a favour because Pickering was short of players.

It was during this period that Matty played in a friendly against FC United and, while having been warned by Josh Howard about the atmosphere, the team spirit and the amazing vocal fans, the occasion still staggered him. In the June he left Woodley Sports and he was persuaded to try out for FC United and earned himself a place in the squad. Matty appeared against Radcliffe Borough and made his senior debut against St Helen's Town and to date has been an ever-present.

He was part of the winning side that wrestled the Supporters Direct Cup away from AFC Wimbledon in July 2006.

Matty Taylor

Football Club United of Manchester

Created from despair - Powered by passion

Television: BBC North West broadcast a half-hour special programme on the birth of FC United on Monday 26th September 2005 at 7.30pm. The programme looked at the reasons behind the birth of the club, and included exclusive behind-the-scenes footage, match action and interviews.

Whilst not fortunate enough to feature on 'Match of the Day', FC United have appeared on a Granada production. The half-hour show was aired on 12th November 2005. Sky News also had brief mentions of FC United on 3rd and 7th January 2006. A local Manchester television and cable station, Channel M, began a regular monthly documentary/action programme about FC United, a team it called "The most famous non-league football club in the UK". The 30-minute programme concentrated on the second half of the season but ran with the club's beginnings and had interviews with the Board, management, fans, players and the dedicated background staff. The show also had match coverage of the January games. The programme began on Monday 30th January at 7pm and was repeated at 10.30pm.

FCUM.TV, accessed from the club's official website, hosts commentary by Roy Williamson and Sam Huddart whilst showing highlights from previous games.

Tickets: Season tickets cost just £112 with the price of under 18s being £32 and OAPs at £80.

Ticket – All: The first all-ticket league game was FC United's first ever league game away to Leek CSOB. FC United's first home game was a turnstile affair and no tickets were sold. The fact that it was an 'All-Ticket' affair also meant that it was the first all-ticket game in the history of the North West Counties Football League. The first all-ticket League Cup game was against Cheadle Town on 15th October 2005 and was restricted to 2,200 by the police.

FC United's first ever Cup Final against Curzon Ashton in the 2006/7 season was also an all-ticket affair.

Torpey, Steve (Forward): Born 16/9/1981 in Liverpool.

Has the honour of scoring FC United's first goal in a friendly against Flixton, which was FC United's third game after 281 minutes without a goal.

Steve attended the Academy of Liverpool, where he played along with Michael Owen between 1998 and 2001 and where he became an England schoolboy international. Once of Prescot Cables, he was their leading goalscorer in the 2002/3 season with 28 goals and where one of his team mates was a certain Dave Chadwick. He played for Wigan, Port Vale, where he went on loan to Scarborough and then Altrincham. At Altrincham he wasn't alone either: Mark Rawlinson and Joz Mitten were among his team mates. Steve has a trademark, a male thong. It was bought for him as a joke one Christmas, allegedly by his mother, and he vowed to show off his thong every time he scored a goal. Steve has continued to 'show off' his thong.

He was employed as a football coach during his spell at FC United and during a pre-season friendly against Halifax Town he scored a beauty and prompted Halifax Town to sign him on professional terms; the first FC United player to do so.

Football Club United of Manchester
Created from despair - Powered by passion

Steve had to return to Gigg Lane to be presented with an award. He was presented with the 'Supporters Network Player of the Year' in August 2006.

Training: The FC United squad and players that the manager wants to have a look at assemble twice a week, Tuesdays and Thursdays, at a nearby club for training and physio.

Trees, Robert (Defender): Born 18/12/1977 in Manchester. Robert went through the youth scheme at Old Trafford and played league football at Bristol Rovers. He played non-league football with his local team, Droylsden, a brief spell at Altrincham, then Leigh RMI, making his debut in November 2000 and appearing 21 times, leaving in 2003. He then joined Mossley during the 2002/3 season with another member of FC United: Tony Coyne. Robert had a spell at Hyde United. He signed en route to a game after a defender phoned in sick and made his debut the same day. Signed for FC United from Abbey Hey FC, but left the club before the season began.

Trials: The Steering Group and Management held public trials at Manchester University on 26th June 2005. Over 900 players of all standards applied, far more than expected and from all corners of the world and far too many to deal with. This number was whittled down to around 205 based on experience. 17 were selected to go forward for pre-season training.

Trophies – The Myra Mandryk Trophy: Myra Mandryk, a legend at Bower Fold for all her hard work on and off the park, had been struck down by severe illness. Stalybridge Celtic began to raise funds in her honour. Karl Marginson and Phil Power, both ex-Celtics heroes, arranged a friendly between Stalybridge Celtic and the newly-formed FCUoM. Stalybridge Celtic won 2-0.

Sadly, Myra passed in 2007 away after losing her battle with cancer.

Turner, Adam (Defender): Born 31/12/86.

Reserve Squad.

Adam was awarded both the Players' 'Player of the Season' and the Manager's 'Player of the Season' awards for the opening 2006/7 season. He is often given the role of captain.

Adam played in the pre-season friendly game that lost to Kirkham and Wesham in July 2006.

U

Undefeated: FC United were undefeated away from home in their inaugural season, winning 13 games and drawing 5, scoring 44 goals and conceding just 17.

During the 2006/7 season, FC United were unbeaten in the league from 2nd December 2006 till the end of the season on 28th April 2007: 22 games, home and away.

Football Club United of Manchester
Created from despair - Powered by passion

V

Vacancies: FC United advertised the vacancies of Chief Executive and Secretary in the *Manchester Evening News* and on the club's website. The positions had been filled in an acting capacity and in keeping with the club's fair recruitment policy advertised the positions. The positions were filled in February 2006 with Andy Walsh becoming Chief Executive, though he and the club were more comfortable with the title General Manager. Luc Zentar was appointed Secretary and he carries on the good work he began as an unpaid secretary.

Varley, Stephen:

Reserve Squad.

Stephen was named in the squad list for the friendly game against Kirkham and Wesham in July 2006.

Vaz Te, Fernando (Midfielder): Born 8/7/85.

Reserve Squad.

Fernando is the older brother of Ricardo Vaz Te, who plies his trade with the Premiership side Bolton Wanderers FC. Fernando signed for FC United in September 2006 and made his debut for the first team in the 7-1 win over Abbey Hey; a few weeks later coming on for hat-trick hero Stuart Rudd and picking up his first yellow card as well. Fernando also played in the pre-season friendly against Kirkham and Wesham in July 2006. Fernando came to the attention of the club through a friend of a friend and impressed during training to become involved. He is a regular in the reserve side, scoring goals from the midfield.

Venues: A number of teams in the NWCFL Division Two and cup opponents have changed venues in order to gain financially from FC United's large travelling fan-base and to secure the safety of fans. FC United have regularly had attendances of over 2,500. The first team to change venue was Winsford United, who moved their fixture from their Bartow Stadium to Northwich Victoria's Victoria Stadium, which has a capacity of 4,000. During FC United's 1st season more than 7 teams have changed venue. Clubs wanting to host the matches in order to gain extra revenue had contacted clubs in the hope that they would switch grounds. FC United's last away game of the season against Padiham was also moved – Padiham using Oldham Athletic's Boundary Park ground.

FC United played one of their home games 'away' from home when Gigg Lane was used for a beer festival, an agreement made prior to FC United ground sharing and FC United using Altrincham's Moss Lane ground instead.

Victories: FC United won 27 of the 36 league games played during their inaugural season, a feat bettered the following season when FC United won 36 league games out of the 42 played.

Biggest: The biggest winning margin was 10-2. FC United put 10 past Castleton Gabriels on 10th December 2005.

Football Club United of Manchester
Created from despair - Powered by passion

W

Website: The official website of FCUoM is:

http://www.fc-utd.co.uk

During the set-up months of FCUoM, a secure website was designed and supporters began to pledge their money to the cause. 2,600 supporters pledged money within a week.

There are many fans' websites and forums on the internet dedicated to FCUoM and many websites around the world have mentioned FC United, including Ajax, the Dutch side.

Weston, Matt (Defender): Born 5/11/1975 in Manchester.

Matt was a professional footballer with his twin brother Kenny at Ipswich Town. Matt also lists Altrincham, Droylsden, Leigh RMI, and FC Locomotiv amongst his previous clubs. Both attended the trials in June. Matt made two appearances in pre-season friendly games and in the squad to play for the Supporters Direct Cup against AFC Wimbledon in July 2005, but is no longer with the club.

Wilson, Eugene (Gus) (Assistant coach to the U18s): Born 11/4/1963 in Manchester.

Gus is brother to Clive Wilson, who played at Spurs and a huge favourite at Crewe. A reliable and dependable defender in his time, Gus was a professional at Crewe Alexandra between August 1994 and May 1995. He played in 115 games, scoring just the one goal, which was later ruled out when Aldershot went broke. His playing days took him to many clubs. The late 1990s saw him playing at Hyde United, where he stayed for a couple of seasons. He took time out and went to America to gain coaching experience and returned early in 2001, when he moved to Radcliffe Borough and in May 2002 he took the first of many coaching roles when he returned to Hyde United as assistant manager/coach. Later that year, he joined Gary Thomas coaching trouble-torn Flixton, before moving on to ply his trade with Winsford United. In 2003 he was at Winsford United, 2004 at Trafford, as well as at Astro. 2004 saw his coaching career pay dividends as he was the coach at Manchester Maccabi Juniors, who joined forces with Manchester City FC, who became the official supplier of junior players to Manchester City. Gus, a EUFA-qualified coach, also gained experience at Old Mancunians AFC and joined Glossop North End as coach in 2006. He left Glossop North End in July 2006 to join the coaching staff at FC United, helping Chris Simms with the juniors.

In May 2007 his coaching skills helped Manchester Grammar School's senior side lift the Manchester Schools Cup with an emphatic 4-1 win over South Manchester's St Bede's College and winning the trophy for the first time since 1996.

Wins:

Successive: FCUoM won their first 3 ever league games. The longest winning streak in the inaugural season was 7 league games with victories over Winsford United (2-1), Darwen (2-0), Nelson (3-1), Ashton Town (2-1), Daisy Hill (3-0), Blackpool

Football Club United of Manchester
Created from despair - Powered by passion

Mechanics (4-2) and Holker Old Boys (4-1) during January and February 2006.

This feat was bettered in the 2006/7 season. FC United won their first 12 games, conceding only 6 goals and scoring 49 in the process, and later on in the season won another 12 games on the bounce from 3rd March to 21st April 2007, scoring 51 goals and conceding just 10.

Home: During the inaugural season, FC United won 11 games at home.

During the 2006/7 season, FC United won 19 home games.

Wolstenholme, Michael (Midfield): Born in Ashton-under-Lyne.

Midfielder Mike Wolstenholme plied his trade with many clubs. He started as a trainee at Crewe Alexandra and lists among his clubs Mossley from around 1996 through to 2003, with loan spells at various clubs in the meantime.

Whilst at Mossley he played alongside Josh Howard, Tony Coyne and Rob Trees, all players he was to meet up again with at FC United. He became Ashton United's longest serving player, having spent 4 years there. He played for Clitheroe before FC United, but he had successful spells at Droylsden, Abbey Hey, Atherton Collieries and after FC United at Woodley Sports.

Mike was listed in the squads for pre-season friendlies 2005/6 for FC United.

Wright, Jerome (Midfielder): Born 29/10/1985 in Wythenshawe.

As an 8-year-old dreaming of playing on the wing like his hero Ryan Giggs, he joined a team called Unity and the team performed well, winning trophies.

Oldham Athletic invited him to join their youth side and he drew great inspiration from watching the professionals training on the pitch next to theirs.

Being of a slightly smaller build than the other players, he was often pitted up against lads who were older and bigger and he relished the challenge, gaining valuable experience playing in tournaments up and down the country and even playing against such accomplished players as Wayne Rooney.

Unfortunately, Oldham let him go aged 16 and he took up a semi career change and enrolled in college, when he was invited to turn out for Maine Road by an 'old' friend of his. Chris Simms liked what he saw in the youngster and persuaded him to sign for them and he flourished under the guidance of Simms.

He went into the first team and in his first season, 2002/3, Maine Road finished third, but he won the club's 'Player of the Year' award and, just as things were looking up on the park, he suffered a serious knee injury that side-lined him for 18 months.

Maine Road stood by the talent and nurtured him back to health, taking it slowly one game at a time and as he regained fitness and confidence Maine Road gained promotion and were doing well in Division One. FC United had also gained promotion in their inaugural season, but Jerome had a different battle.

He was trying to represent England in a tournament, vying for a place against 3,000 other hopefuls and by a series of elimination games he made the final 8.

Football Club United of Manchester
Created from despair - Powered by passion

The team was managed by Jamie Redknapp and the team performed well, finishing third, with Harry Redknapp checking in on his son occasionally and the team pleading for trials at Portsmouth falling on deaf ears!

Jerome returned to Maine Road, scoring 9 goals in 25 outings before his transfer to Gigg Lane.

This talented left-sided midfielder was bought in to restore the balance after Steve Torpey left to join Halifax Town. FC United put a seven-day request in for Wright, who had been out for 18 months with an injury. Maine Road were reluctant to see him go that December 2006. Jerome made his away debut on 6th January 2007 in the 3-0 win over Atherton Collieries and his home debut in the 3-2 win over Curzon Ashton on 21st February 2007. He earned his first yellow card in the hard-fought 1-1 draw against Nantwich Town three days later. 3rd March 2007 saw Wright score his first FC goal at home against Colne in the 6-2 win and he scored his second FC goal 5 minutes later.

Jerome helped FC United to book their place in the UniBond with a 2-1 win over Ramsbottom, a game in which he scored.

Previous clubs include Griffin Growlers.

X

On football pools, X stands for draws. During FCUoM's first season there were only 6 drawn games and all but one of these came away from home.

During the two seasons in the NWCFL, FC United drew 10 games in total.

Y

Yellow Cards: The first yellow card issued in a home league game went to Tony Coyne. He was booked in the first half against Padiham for dissent after arguing with the referee. Adie Orr was booked during the second half. The first yellow card in an away game and indeed the first player to receive a yellow card went to Joz Mitten for celebrating his goal against Leek CSOB. Ray Notice of Eccleshall has the unfortunate tag of being the first player to be cautioned playing against FC United for a foul on Tony Coyne. During the home defeat to Norton United, 4 FC United players were awarded yellows: keeper Barrie George, Rob Nugent, Steve Torpey and substitute Joz Mitten.

In the 2006/7 season, FC United's players amassed a total of 63 yellow cards: 52 league and 11 cup, with Rory Patterson getting 9 alone.

Youngest Player: The youngest player to play for FC United's 1st team was Will Ahern, aged 18 years.

Youth Team: As part of FCUoM's policy, the club has begun looking into a youth team for the 2006/7 season, with manager Karl Marginson involved in the progression of the youngsters.
The side played in the North West Youth Alliance league (NWYA).

Youth Team Players:
Immi Arain (Defender): A confident defender, Immi wears

personalised boots on the park and enjoys life off it. He is a skilled player who includes Castleton Gabriels and Norden FC as his previous clubs. He has tasted success, winning a cup final and being voted man of the match.

David Brook: David is listed in FC United's programme as a youth team member.

Rob Calderbank (Defender): Rob was born in Manchester and is a Manchester United fan to boot. Rob plays for the youth side and could soon be pushing for a place in the reserves. Previous clubs include Sale Juniors. Rob was named in the winning squad for the reserve cup final in May 2007.

Rymel Downer (Midfielder): Rymel is listed in FC United's programme as a youth team member.

Russell Guffogg (Defender): Russell previously played for Seedfield Sports Club, with whom he won a league title. He played in the 4-1 loss to Altrincham Youth in September 2006.

Johnny Hall (Defender/midfielder): He is one of the youngest members of the side and is a very capable defender or midfielder. Has high ambitions and is looking forward to great success at Gigg Lane playing in the first team. Previous clubs include Cheadle and Gatley St James.

Andy Harrison: Andy is listed in FC United's programme as a youth team member.

Liam Hayes: Liam is listed in FC United's programme as a youth team member.

Mark Hendstock (Forward): Like some of his team mates, Mark has also experienced the winning feeling. Playing for Northend Boys U16s, his scoring ability helped the team to retain their league title for the second year running. His prowess in front of goal has also seen him play his part as he scored in the 5-1 demolition of Prescot Cables, FC United's biggest competitive win.

Danny Hulme: Danny is listed in FC United's programme as a youth team member.

Liam James (Midfielder):   Born in Rochdale and an ex-Liverpool junior,   Liam is a Manchester City fan who has scored a goal at the Kop End at Anfield.

Philip Leaff (Goalkeeper): Born 11/12/1988. Phil is a very promising young goalkeeper signed for FC United in June 2006 and making his debut in the friendly game against Flint Town on 8th July 2006.   Only 17-years-old, but he showed excellent maturity for his years in keeping a clean sheet. Previously in the Altrincham Youth side. Phil played in the opening game of the season for the reserves and kept a clean sheet in the 7-0 thrashing of Padiham in August 2006.

Reynaldo Mike: Reynaldo is listed in FC United's programme as a youth team member.

Vidal Mike (Forward): Vidal is one of the younger members of the side, following in his older brother Leon's footsteps, who plied his trade north of the border before joining FC United and, like his brother, is a Manchester City fan.   He once played for renowned side Fletcher Moss. He played in the 4-1 loss to Altrincham Youth in September 2006.

Anthony O'Neil (Defender): He played in the 4-1 loss to Altrincham Youth in September 2006 and was in the winning squad for the reserve cup final in May 2007.

Anthony Roberts: Anthony is listed in FC United's programme as a youth team member.

Jamie Rother (Midfielder): Played in a mid-season friendly against Warrington Town for the 1st team and impressed the manager. The team won 5-1. Awarded the Manager's 'Player of the Season' award for 2006/7. Jamie has progressed to make appearances for the reserves. He played in the 4-1 loss to Altrincham Youth in September 2006 and was named in the winning squad for the reserve cup final in May 2007.

Callum Rothwell (Forward): Australian-born Callum plied his trade with Duninfield Youth and Town and has scored in the winning side to lift the Manchester County Cup. He played in the 4-1 loss to Altrincham Youth in September 2006.

Dominic Stockdale (Midfielder): Dominic has tasted the joys of winning a trophy. Playing for Moston Junior U15s, he scored a goal in the 5-0 thrashing of Westbury Sports and helped to lift the Manchester County FA Youth Cup. As well as playing regularly for the youth side, he has captained the side and has progressed to make appearances for the reserves. He captained the youth side in the 4-1 loss to Altrincham Youth in September 2006. Dominic was named in the winning squad for the reserve cup final in May 2007.

Michael Sullivan: Youth player Sully played in the mid-season friendly against Woodley Sports for the first team and had an excellent goal ruled out by the referee's assistant. He played in the 4-1 loss to Altrincham Youth in September 2006.

Tony Tompos (Goalkeeper): Tony was awarded the Player's 'Player of the Season' in 2006/7.

Z

Zenith: The high point of FC United's inaugural season was winning the Division Two title at the first time of asking and being promoted as champions. Winning the Division One League title and League Challenge Cup double in the 2006/7 season rank highly in their list of achievements.

FC United avenged their defeat to AFC Wimbledon in the Supporters Direct Cup by winning 2-1 to add to their silverware.

FC United became the third best supported non-league football club in the world with an average of 3,059 fans behind FC Lokomotive Leipzig and Exeter City.

Josh Howard congratulated.

Players used in the 2005/6 season:

Goalkeepers: Barrie George, Philip Melville.

Defenders: Dave Chadwick, Dave Brown, Billy McCartney,
                Gareth Ormes, Rob Nugent, William Collier, Tony

Football Club United of Manchester

Created from despair - Powered by passion

	Cullen, Kev Elvin.
Midfield:	Josh Howard, Ryan Gilligan, Tony Coyne, Matt Hayley, Ryan Hevicon, Steve Spencer, Simon Carden, Mike O'Neill, Will Ahern, Mark Rawlinson, Chris Simms, David Swarbrick.
Strikers:	Joz Mitten, Rory Patterson, Leon Mike, Adie Orr, Simon Band, Steve Torpey, Stuart Rudd, Scott Holt.

Players used in the 2006/7 season:

Goalkeepers:	Sam Ashton, John Ogden.
Defenders:	Dave Chadwick, Dave Brown, Liam Coyne, Alex Mortimer, Rob Nugent, Matthew Taylor, Shaun Roscoe.
Midfielders:	Simon Carden, Rhodri Giggs, Joshua Howard, Nicky Platt, Gary Sampson, Steve Smith, Steve Spencer, Dave Swarbrick, Jerome Wright.
Strikers:	Rory Patterson, Jamie Phoenix, Stuart Rudd.

References used

www.fc-utd.co.uk

Fc United Programmes

www.bookrags.com

www.wikipedia.com

The Gladwish land sales Ultimate book of Non League players
2004-05

www.bury.co.uk

www.altrincham.co.uk

www.manchesteronline.co.uk

www.hydeunited.il2.com

www.ask.com

http://punkfootball.wordpress.com

The Cherry Red Non League News desk Annual.

www.burytimes.co.uk

www.forevermanutd.com

www.tonykempster.co.uk

www.bujold.co.uk

http://www.salfordadvertiser.co.uk

http://www.footballtransfers.co.uk

http://mysite.wanadoo-members.co.uk

http://www.soccerbase.com

http://www.nonleaguedaily.com

http://www.unibondleague.com

http://www.google.co.uk

http://www.ask.co.uk

Printed in the United Kingdom by
Lightning Source UK Ltd., Milton Keynes
R973400001B/R9734PG137815UKX16B/7/A